THE BELLSBURG MITCHELLS

THE BELLSBURG MITCHELLS

A Genealogical Journey

BRIAN PATRICK MITCHELL

PONTIC PRESS

ALEXANDRIA, VIRGINIA

2022

THE BELLSBURG MITCHELLS
A Genealogical Journey

Pontic Press
P.O. Box 1
Alexandria, VA 22313

www.ponticpress.com

PAPERBACK ISBN: 978-0-9910169-1-4

Buy online: https://www.lulu.com/en/us/shop/brian-patrick-mitchell/the-bellsburg-mitchells/paperback/product-ne7qn8.html

Cover photo: The family of Benjamin Wesley Mitchell, circa 1912.
Front row, seated, L-R: Ruby Morton Greer, Thelma Mitchell, Buford Mitchell, Guysell Mitchell, Tillman Mitchell, Ozell Mitchell.
Second row, children: Russell Matlock, Louise Matlock, Thedford Mitchell.
Third row, seated: Wayne Matlock, Benjamin Wesley Mitchell, Allie Fry Mitchell, Ida Morton.
Fourth row, standing: Fate Mitchell, Myrtle Mitchell Matlock, Vera Morton Mitchell, James Mitchell, Nancy Morton Mitchell, Lester Mitchell, Cora Mitchell (daughter of Dave Mitchell), Rufus Mitchell.

Fig. 1, "The Right Man for the Right Place," Niday Picture Library / Alamy Stock Photo, used with permission.

To my father

John Tillman Mitchell, Jr.

to whom the greater credit goes

for all that follows.

*"Show me the manner in which a nation
or a community cares for its dead,
and I will measure with mathematical exactness
the tender sympathies of its people,
their respect for the laws of the land,
and their loyalty to high ideals."*

William Gladstone

Table of Contents

Index of Figures

Preface

History is an inheritance we are obliged to learn, respect, preserve, and pass on for the sake of ourselves and others both living and yet to come. Folklore is a form of history not fundamentally different from the history of history books, serving the same purpose in our lives in helping us make sense of our world and our place in it.

Genealogy is form of folklore, a study of the history of particular people descended from other people. The Old English word *lar,* whence *lore,* meant "knowledge." Knowledge is learned, and in fact the words *lore* and *learn* are cognates, both deriving from the Indo-European root *leis-* meaning "footprint." Lore, like a footprint, tells you where you have been, which tells you where you are headed. Without it, you are lost, you are *delirious*—another cognate of *lore,* this one from the Latin word *lira* meaning a furrow, a straight track through a field.[1] To be delirious is to be off track.

One can make too much of genealogy, but one can also make too little of it. There are those who think of nothing beyond their own lives, neither what has gone before them nor what will come after them, and there are those who plainly hate the past for having produced their intolerable present. The former pass by the monuments to our past without noticing them; the latter pull them down and replace them with monuments to themselves. Both are now disastrously off track.

One value of genealogy is that it connects us to the past in a deeply sympathetic way, associating the people of the past with the people of

---

[1] Not to be confused with the Italian word *lira* from the Latin word *libra* meaning "balance, measure."

our present whom we know and love. We learn to see the people of the past not as faceless abstractions but as fathers and mothers. We learn also to see others around us not as just kith but also kin because they share the same past, the same ancestors, and so often the same names. The more genealogy we know, the more people we can call cousins, and that is a good thing. Genealogy is about making connections, not dividing people into groups. The farther back you go, the fewer divisions exist. We all end up as collateral descendants sharing common male and female ancestors, an Adam and an Eve.

Genealogy also teaches us a lot about history, and it does so in a frankly honest way. You learn basic facts about life on the frontier, with its contrast of savagery and civilization, facts that are often absent from big-picture accounts of political and military events. You sometimes learn things about your ancestors you would rather not have learned. You also sometimes learn things that do not fit the dominant historical narrative of the present, which today is plainly Marxist in that it skews its relation of the facts of history ideologically to stress the themes of oppression and injustice at the expense of all other meaning, so as to favor some people over other people, supposed victims over supposed oppressors.

Genealogy is not the sum of knowledge or the key to our existence. It is not in any way determinative of how we should live now and certainly should not be used to divide or condemn people. One still needs to know something of theology and philosophy to put genealogy it into proper perspective. Genealogy can be a foolish waste of time spent on trivial matters of little relevance, but so can history, so can astronomy, so can ornithology, so can any art or science. We need not all study genealogy just as we need not all study birds, but the arcane, trivial, seemingly vain and meaningless work of genealogists can sometimes contribute pieces of knowledge that broaden and deepen our understanding of ourselves and our world.

My time spent on genealogy has been both enjoyable and frustrating. A major attraction of genealogy is the intellectual challenge of a historical mystery. A major frustration is that the mystery is never ending. Just when you think you have figured things out, you stumble across something that confounds your conclusions and raises even more questions requiring more research. Years of research can yield nothing, not even a good stopping point, since there are always other places to look for clues. Even now, there are records I would like to check, and yet I have already spent much more time on this than I intended and am anxious to get on to more important work.

This present work expands upon my earlier unpublished work from 2003 to include the surprising results of a DNA test I took in the fall of 2020 and what I have learned since then in trying to make sense of the test's results. The earlier work is included in this work in its entirety, with a few minor changes and one significant revision worth noting here: In the earlier work, I drew conclusions about my great-great-grandfather Jack Mitchell's political preferences based on his naming his first son Millard Fillmore Mitchell; those conclusions have since proven somewhat inaccurate and have been corrected in this present work (see pp. 5–8). Otherwise, I am pleased to say that my earlier work was surprisingly sound in its use of the evidence available to me at the time and that it is still worth reading as part of this work, even though chapters 2 and 3 tend to toward conclusions different from those of chapters 4 and 5, which are based on DNA and new documentary evidence.

I am indebted to many people for their contributions to my research, analysis, and conclusions, most of all my father, the late John Tillman Mitchell Jr., who began the search and taught me how to continue it, and then my sister Dianne Peters, whose interest in genealogy led her to our first cousin once removed Don Mitchell, who later passed along the name of Larry Mitchell of Michigan, who was looking for Mitchells to take the FamilyTreeDNA test I took in 2020. My fifth cousin James C. Mitchell of Robertson County had already taken one of FamilyTreeDNA's yDNA tests and passed along to me key facts about the Mitchells of Robertson County collected by him and another fifth cousin, the late Colonel Robert Wayne "Bob" Mitchell, who was also of Robertson County and who had also taken one of FamilyTreeDNA's yDNA tests. James also put me in touch with W. Ray Walker, who has spent many of his 94 years documenting the Mitchells of the Robertson County, with the benefit of having known and consulted his great-uncle George Franklin Mitchell, who was born in 1869 and died 1970 at the age of 101. Three members of FamilyTreeDNA's Ralston Project—Ed Ralston, Gordon Rolston, and Mort Rolleston—were also extremely helpful in helping me make sense of the exceedingly complex DNA evidence, which I still do not understand well. Janie Sherman, a professional genealogist in Staunton, Virginia, contributed key documentary evidence from August County records, bringing my investigation to a satisfactory conclusion. Several siblings and cousins contributed generously to the placement of a new headstone for our great-great-grandfather Jack, on a promise from me that I would provide them a revised account of our ancestry. This volume fulfills that promise.

None of the above bear any responsibility for the mistakes made herein, which are mine alone. I doubt I will ever spend much more time on genealogy, but I would welcome additional information, questions, and corrections concerning anything in this volume. Anyone wishing to contact me may do so through my blog at brianpatrickmitchell.com. Anyone desiring additional copies of this volume may ordered them online from Lulu.com at the web address on the copyright page.

Alexandria, Virginia
April 8, 2022

2003 Preface

My name is Brian Patrick Mitchell, my father was John Tillman Mitchell, Jr., and his father was John Tillman Mitchell, Sr. Until I was nearly thirty years old, I could go no further.

Like most Americans, my family paid little attention to its own ancestry. We kept up with the extended family but rarely talked of where it came from—someplace outside Nashville called "the country," which we children later came to know as Dickson and Cheatham Counties. Our elders told stories of their own lives, but I can remember just one that had been handed down from long ago: When the Union Army rushed up the Cumberland River in 1862, and Yankee soldiers came foraging up Sam's Creek in Cheatham County, the menfolk hid themselves and their horses in the hollows, while the women hid the hams beneath the floorboards of their houses. I remember my grandmother, Alma Mitchell, saying, with a gleam in her eye and a grin on her face, "Those Yankees stomped all over those hams but didn't find 'em."

That story defined the only part of the family identity we took from the past: We were Southerners—or Rebels as we children called ourselves—not "damned Yankees" (the only use of a curse word we were allowed). We were also Tennesseans, which seemed somehow better than being Kentuckians, Ohioans, or Virginians. Beyond that, we were Americans and not Communists. And we were Christians, members of the Church of Christ. We believed the Bible and took seriously St. Paul's dismissal of "endless genealogies" in 1 Timothy 1:4. I still do.

But changing times have cast doubt on what it means to be an American, a Tennessean, a Southerner, and a Christian. Others in this country define these terms very differently, often with hostile intent, and many of us have been forced to rethink who we are and where we come from.

I myself began to wonder about our ancestry in 1985. While with the Army in Turkey, I had the chance take my wife to England and Scotland on leave. We stayed with friends near London and then took a train up to Scotland, where we discovered that there is a Mitchell tartan and a Mitchell crest. The tartan is a variation of the blue-and-green Black Watch tartan and is worn today the U.S. Air Force Pipe Band in honor of General Billy Mitchell (no known relation). The crest shows a hand holding a quill pen, with the motto FAVANTE DEO SUPERO—"By God's favor, I prevail." (There are other Mitchell crests and mottos, but this is the one most often marketed and my preference as a writer and a Christian.)

I confess that for a few months afterward I dearly wanted to be Scottish, and as soon as I could I asked my father where our Mitchells came from. England, he answered, and so died a silly dream. But he was not so certain and later confessed that he had answered England "for no other reason whatsoever than the knowledge that there were presently lots of Mitchells in England." Indeed, there were, though there were also lots of Mitchells in Scotland, where it is among the top twenty surnames.

My father would later write that I "pressed" him to look into the matter. I don't recall pressing. I do recall my surprise when I learned months later that he was digging into family history. He had seemed so uninterested when I first asked about it. Later he confessed to me that he had felt ashamed at not knowing more. He began asking questions of relatives and soon found himself hooked. Genealogy became his hobby, and he pursued it until the spring of 1989, when he fell ill with cancer.

In four years, he was able to fill in quite a few blanks. But he was never able to trace the Mitchells across the Atlantic, or even with certainty across the Appalachians. From what he did find, and from what I have been able to add, it is possible that they came from Scotland, though if they had they would have been lowland Scots, who are really a mix of Scottish, English, and other. But it is more likely that they came from England, for reasons that will be explained herein. My father did trace other ancestors to England, as well as to France, Germany, and Ireland. We can also assume Wales for those ancestors with

Welsh names like *Davis*, and Scotland for those ancestors with Scottish names like *Haile* and *Stewart* (though some Stewarts were originally English Stewards).

Further research with the aid of the Internet, which my father did not have, has extended the links he established to the earliest days of the American colonies from New England to South Carolina, and to specific towns in England, Holland, France, and Switzerland. Our first known ancestor to settle in America was Stephen Deane, who arrived in Plymouth Colony in 1621. Another ancestor, William Ring, would have arrived in 1620 with the Mayflower, but poor William was aboard the Mayflower's sister ship, the Speedwell, which sprang a leak and was forced to turn back, leaving the Mayflower to make the journey alone. (More on the Rings and Deanes later.)

My father approached genealogy as a great detective mystery. The challenge was to establish the hereditary links between the generations, which meant a painstaking hunt for historical clues and rigorous testing of hypothetical relations. It wasn't enough for him that a William Mitchell appeared here and then a William Mitchell appeared there; he had to have some reason to relate the two. There were, after all, many William Mitchells.

He was not making up a family mythology. The fun for him was figuring things out. The downside to this approach for us is that, alas, he did not bother to record the many stories he heard from aged kin who have now passed on. The upside is that the connections he did establish can be counted as proved. What he could not prove, he did not claim.

Some of his findings have been widely distributed. This I know from personal experience. When in Nashville in 1990, I was cited for making an improper U-turn at the junction of two country roads. The junction happened to be within the Brentwood city limits. When I went to pay my ticket at the Brentwood city hall, I noticed that the officer behind the counter was also named Mitchell. "Are you from around here?" I asked.

"All my life," he answered.

"Then maybe we're related," I ventured hopefully.

"Let me see," he said. Opening the drawer beneath the counter, he then took out (as if it had been right there on top) a photocopy of the family tree my father had drawn up by hand the year before he died.

The officer, whose first name I have forgotten, was the grandson of Jerry Lester Mitchell, one of my grandfather's older brothers. That made us second cousins. (I still paid the ticket. We Mitchells are honest folk.)

Lord willing and my hands hold out, I will someday write an apology for paying attention to our ancestry—and a warning to those who would make too much of it. For now, please accept the following as a small piece of self-knowledge, a blessing for those who rightly believe, a temptation for those who do not.

CHAPTER 1

In Search of Jack Mitchell

My father J.T. Mitchell started his inquiry into the family history by talking to his mother Alma in Ashland City and then his other known Mitchell kin in Tennessee, including some who had known his father Tillman as a boy. "Most of the Mitchell family know or knew very little about my Great-grandfather John Tillman (Jack) Mitchell except his legendary temper," he wrote to me in 1986. My father himself did not know starting out that Jack's full name was his own. Grandmother Alma knew this and assumed that my father knew it, too. She told me later of her surprise at finding out otherwise. (It happens all too often that elders assume their children receive and remember every memory their elders hold dear, but how can they unless a deliberate effort is made to pass such things on?)

Grandmother also knew the names of most of Jack's children (twelve in all, by two wives). From 94-year-old Herschel Speight, my father learned that Jack's first wife was a Speight and his second wife was a Taylor. In fact, Jack's first wife was Herschel's aunt, though Herschel could not remember her first name. My father also talked to Grady Mitchell, who ran the Mitchell bait shop in the Bellsburg area of Dickson County, where so many Mitchells grew up. My father wrote to me in 1986:

> [Grady] is about my age and Mama had remembered his dad as having taught singing in that area, but I was sure that our relationship was somewhat distant.
>
> Grady said that his dad had always told him that they were related to Jack and to all those other Mitchell's around there

1

that ended their names in "HELL" (meaning 2 L's). He always said that they were Scotch-Irish who came over the mountains from N.C. on mules.

The only other information my father had to go on were the dates on the tombstones of his grandparents in the yard of the Mt. Liberty Presbyterian Church in Bellsburg: Ben West Mitchell (born 17 July 1863, died 14 July 1916) and Allie Fry Mitchell (born 17 April 1870, died 9 July 1934).

My father had been told that Jack Mitchell was buried in the same churchyard, but in his many visits to the church he had never seen the grave. After talking to the old folks, he went back to look again. The first thing he noticed was that the empty spaces between marked graves weren't always empty spaces. They were graves with old flat headstones hidden beneath the overgrown grass and fallen leaves. As he wrote in his notes:

> Crawling on hands and knees, pulling up grass, and digging with my fingers, I uncovered (and I mean literally uncovered) the grave marker:
>
> Jack Mitchell
> 1827   1899

He also uncovered several stones marked "UNKNOWN" before finding others with the names Grandmother had given him for Jack's offspring. Only then did he begin to consult official records of surrounding counties and the U.S. Census. In time, he would fill in all the names and dates of Jack's family. He would also, with confidence, take his knowledge of Jack's line back one more generation, to William and Mary Mitchell, Jack's father and mother. Had he lived longer, into the age of the Internet, my father might have gone much further, but let us hear what he could say with certainty, before considering where his search might have taken him today.

◆

There were many William Mitchells in Middle Tennessee in the early nineteenth century, but our William Mitchell first appears in 1812 in

Robertson County. His name is on the 1812 tax list and the 1812 Justice-of-the-Peace list in Robertson. He also signed a petition in Robertson that year, opposing the building of a jail in Springfield, the county seat.

William first appears in census records for Robertson County in 1820 and is listed then as between the ages of 26 and 45, so he must have been born before 1794. If he was of full legal age (21) in 1812, he would have been born in 1791. With him in 1820 are his wife in the same age range, a female under 10, a male under 10, another female under 10, and one slave. Their ages allowed my father to track the same William to a listing in the 1830 census for Dickson County. By then, the family had added three more females and one more male, all under five. The young male is Jack, born John Tillman Mitchell in 1827.

William last appears in census records in 1840, between the ages of 40 and 50. His eldest son, William M., is listed separately with his young bride, Surrena Speight (m. Jan. 24, 1840), who is between 15 and 20. Jack, at 13, is still in his father's house, where there is another young male under 5, Jack's younger brother Benjamin (b. 1837).

In 1850, Mary Mitchell is listed as the head of the household. She is 58 and was born in North Carolina in 1792. John (Jack) Mitchell, 23 years old, is the man of the house. Emily is 20. Benjamin is 13. Adaline Andrews (nee Mitchell, b. 1819) is 30 and has three children of her own in Mary's house (Benjamin, William J., and Martha E.). William Milton Mitchell and his wife Surrena (nee Speight) are still on their own. He is 33, she is 24, and their four sons are 10 or under (William D., James M., Albert S., and John W.). Elizabeth Mitchell has married Aaron Pinson in 1844, and they have a daughter, 5, and two younger sons.

In 1860, on the eve of the Civil War, Mary's house is almost empty. Her daughter E.J. (Emily) is still at home at 27. Benjamin's still there at 22. "J.T. Mitchell" (Jack) and his sister Adaline Andrews have left home and are listed separately in the 1860 census. Mary is 68. Her land is valued at $300, and her personal estate is valued at $400, all a widow might need with a grown son next door. Jack is listed just before Mary in the census, recorded on the same day, October 21. He is 36 and a farmer, with land valued at $700 and a personal estate valued

3

at $1,000. He and his wife Martha A., 23, have three young daughters and a year-old son, Millard F.[2]

Jack's older brother, Wm. M. Mitchell, has gotten the greater share of their father's inheritance. In 1860, he is 47 and a farmer, with land valued at $1,000, and a personal estate valued at $2,750. Slaves likely made up most of the difference in personal estate, but this information does not appear in the census of "Free Inhabitants."[3]

We can tell from the census that Jack and William are both humble farmers because the listing just before Jack is "M. Bell Jr.," who is 28 and a farmer with $10,000 in land and $28,275 in personal estate. Jack's next-door neighbor happens to be the richest man in the county, the son of Montgomery Bell Sr., owner of the Cumberland Furnace, who made his fortune casting cannonballs for General Andrew Jackson.

Bellsburg was named for Montgomery Bell Sr. It was originally Bellville but became Bellsburgh in 1849 when the community got its first post office. (Tennessee already had a Bellville post office in Roane County.) Bellsburgh became Bellsburg in 1884.[4] Never much of a town, the settlement originally stretched upland from the mouth of the Harpeth River, where a ferry operated as early as 1805. Records show that the will of Mary Ann Bell, sister of Montgomery Bell Sr., was "Signed at the mouth of Harpeth River 5 Feb. 1847." Records from 1849 show that Aaron Pinson, who married Elizabeth Mitchell in 1844, bought "two lots in the town of Bellville for the sum of 35 dollars." These lots were "laid off by Montgomery Bell, just below the mouth of the Harpeth River."

Aaron Pinson was killed in 1862 at Fort Donelson while serving in Company G, 50th Tennessee Infantry. He was 46. In 1870, his widow

---

[2] The 1860 census record for Jack Mitchell is viewable online at http://www.rootsweb.com/~usgenweb/tn/dickson/census/1860/0287b.gif.

[3] The 1860 census page for William M. Mitchell is viewable online at http://www.rootsweb.com/~usgenweb/tn/dickson/census/1860/0286a.gif.

[4] Like the German word *burg*, meaning "castle," the Old English word *burgh* or *burh* meant a fortified place, be it a town like Edinburgh in Scotland or a ford like Burford in Oxfordshire.

Elizabeth told the census taker that she was 45 years old, when in fact she was ten years older. Her brother J.T. Mitchell is listed as Jack in the 1870 census. His wife Martha has died, and the 43-year-old Jack has married 16-year-old Henrietta Taylor on July 3, 1870. Jack has three teenage daughters at home (Sarah, Bettie, and Rena) and three younger sons: ten-year-old Millard, eight-year-old David, and six-year-old Benjamin.

The names of Jack's sons tell us a lot about him. David was actually Jefferson Davis Mitchell and is listed as "Jif Davis" in the 1880 census. He was born in 1861 and named in honor of the president of Jack's new country, the Confederate States of America. Benjamin was Benjamin Wesley Mitchell, or Ben West as he was later known. He was born in July 1863 and bears the names of his father's kid brother Benjamin and his mother's brother Wesley Speight. That much is unremarkable: family names and a famous name of the day, demonstrating perhaps little more than Jack's support of the Confederacy.

But what about Jack's eldest son? Millard's full name was Millard Fillmore Mitchell. Why would Jack name his first son after former President Millard Fillmore? Did he just like famous names? But there were many more famous names to pick from in December 1859, when Millard Mitchell was born. The president at the time was James Buchanan, and before him there had been Franklin Pierce. Fillmore had not been president since 1853. He had only become president because Zachary Taylor died in office, and he served as president for just three years. Yet Jack was still thinking quite highly of him five years later, so highly that he named his first son and heir after him. What did Jack know about Fillmore that we don't?

Millard Fillmore came from a poor family in upstate New York. Largely self-taught, he got his start in politics as a candidate of the Anti-Mason Party. The Anti-Masons were a reform-minded party of concerned Christians alarmed by the growing influence of Freemasons in politics and business. Freemasonry was and is a secret cult of pretended enlightenment, a vaguely deistic and syncretic religion that is fundamentally hostile to orthodox Christianity. In the 1820's, Masons in upstate New York murdered a disaffected Mason who had threatened to reveal their secrets. The Anti-Mason Party arose amid the popular outrage sparked by the crime.

Fillmore was elected as an Anti-Mason to the New York state legislature and the U.S. House of Representatives. In New York, he sponsored a bill to end imprisonment for nonpayment of debt. In the House, he aligned himself with the Whig Party against Andrew Jackson's Democrats. He was against slavery but feared the abolitionists would tear the country apart. He also opposed open immigration, which some Northern Whigs favored for economic and political reasons. In 1848, the Whigs picked Fillmore to balance their presidential ticket, headed by a pro-slavery Southerner, General Zachary Taylor. When Taylor died in office, Fillmore pushed through the Compromise of 1850. This endeared him to Southerners but hardened Northern Whigs against him. In 1852, he lost the Whig nomination for president to General Winfield Scott, who lost the election to Democrat Franklin Pierce.

But Fillmore wasn't finished. In 1856, he ran for president as the candidate of both the shrinking Whig Party and the new American Party, which began life as a nativist movement derided by rivals as the "Know-Nothings" but quickly evolved into a populist alternative to politics as usual. In 1856, politics as usual pitted the dominant economic interests of the North against the dominant economic interests of the South. The Democratic Party represented Big Business and Big Banking in the South based on the mass production and the trans-Atlantic export of agricultural goods, chiefly cotton and tobacco, supported by slave labor and low tariffs on manufactured goods imported from Europe. The new Republican Party represented Big Business and Big Banking in the North based on the mass production of manufactured goods for domestic consumption, supported by a constant influx of cheap immigrant labor, chiefly Irish Catholics fleeing the Potato Famine, and high tariffs on goods imported from Europe, a trade policy known as mercantilism. The American Party and the Whig Party represented the people in the middle: Northerners threatened by low wages and changing demographics, Southerners threatened by mercantilism and abolitionism, and patriots everywhere threatened by secessionism and civil war. Together, the two parties stood for national unity and peace through continued compromise between North and South.

Fillmore was not the ineffectual, xenophobic mediocrity of myopic postmodern history. He was actually quite popular after leaving the White House, not just welcomed but feted throughout the U.S. and Europe. He left the White House as a successful president if unsuccessful presidential candidate, having accomplished his main aim as president, which was to keep the Union together at a time when it seemed certain to break apart. That this aim cost him reelection shows how close the country already was to civil war. In April 1851, Fillmore wrote to a cousin, "The darkest day of my life was the day of General Taylor's death. The event was so sudden I was wholly unprepared for it. The country seemed on the verge of revolution."[5]

THE RIGHT MAN FOR THE RIGHT PLACE.

Figure 1

[5] Quoted by Robert J. Scarry, *Millard Fillmore* (Jefferson, N.C.: McFarland, 2001), p. 171.

In the presidential election of 1856, Fillmore's national unity ticket proved more popular in the South than in the North. Democrat James Buchanan won the election with 19 states, defeating Republican John C. Fremont, who won 11 states. Fillmore won only Maryland, but he polled over 40 percent in the Deep South and over 48 percent in the five border states: Delaware, Maryland, Kentucky, Tennessee, and Missouri.[6] He won 14 counties in Middle Tennessee, including Davidson and Williamson Counties with over 60 percent and Robertson and Montgomery Counties with over 50 percent. He narrowly lost Cheatham County to Buchanan, 52 to 48 percent (465 to 423).

Now we know why Jack Mitchell named his first son after Millard Fillmore. Fillmore was still alive and well in December 1859, when Jack's first son was born. Jack might have hoped Fillmore would run again for president in 1860, or he might simply have wanted to declare his political preference for unity, compromise, stability, and peace in advance of a viciously divisive and ultimately disastrous election. Jack therefore named his first son born in 1859 after his political hero, Millard Fillmore; his second son born in 1861 after his new president, Jefferson Davis; and his third son born in 1863 after close kin, his younger brother Benjamin Mitchell and his wife's brother Wesley Speight.[7] Why kin? Because in 1862, the Union Army under U.S. Grant swept up the Cumberland to Nashville, spoiling the land along the way. Jack's farm along the river would not have been spared. Ben West's 1863 birthplace was again part of the United States, and his father for at least a time had given up politics.

Little else is known about Jack Mitchell. His brother "Milt" appears later as a delegate to the Democratic Party's state convention, but Jack's post-war politics are a mystery. He was remembered chiefly for his fierce temper. Considering all that he had hoped for and lost, that's hardly surprising. The only story I heard tell of Jack's temper concerned his attempt to get a mule across a ford in the Harpeth River.

---

[6] Robert J. Rayback, *Millard Fillmore: Biography of a President* (Newtown, Conn.: American Political Biography Press, 2009), p. 413.
[7] Naming children after siblings was quite common in those days. Namesake aunts and uncles served as godparents and guardians and were expected to favor the children named for them in their wills.

The mule was taking its ease in the cooling waters of the river, and nothing Jack did could get it to move. An exasperated Jack at last gave up and left the river for the far bank, where he lay down in the ruts of the road, covering his face with his hat.

Jack Mitchell lay down for good in 1899 and was buried at the Mt. Liberty Presbyterian Church, next to his second wife Henrietta (whose headstone still says "Henry Mitchell"). To Heniretta's left are their daughters Lura and Nona, who died very young, and Jack's sister Elizabeth "Betty" Pinson; to Jack's right are their sons Walter Lee (1889–1914) and Clyde L. (1893–1915). Sons Dave and Ben West Mitchell are buried elsewhere in the cemetery; Son Millard is buried at the Mitchell family graveyard on South Harpeth Road in Davidson County. Below is my father's final listing of his Bellsburg kin:

(1) William Mitchell, b. b/n 1791 and 1794, d. before 1850, and Mary *Margaret Stewart?*, 1792–

(2) Elizabeth, 1815–1892
(2) William Milton, 1817–
(2) Adaline, 1819–
(2) *Mary?*
(2) *Martha?*
(2) John Tillman, 1827–1899, and 1. Martha A. Speight, 1832–

(2) Emily J., 1830–
(2) Benjamin, 1837–

   (3) M.E. (Betty), 1853–1924
   (3) M.A. (Rena), 1855–1933
   (3) Millard Fillmore, 1858–1933
   (3) Jefferson Davis, 1861–1941
   (3) Benjamin Wesley, 1863–1916, and Sally Allie Fry, 1870–1934

2. Henrietta Taylor, 1852–1911
   (3) Lela, 1872–1971
   (3) John Norris, 1874–
   (3) Martha (Mattie), 1876–1913
   (3) Lura, 1879–
   (3) J. Herman, 1881–1949
   (3) Nona
   (3) Walter Lee, 1889–1914
   (3) Clyde L., 1893–1915

      (4) Myrtle Lela, 1886–1963
      (4) James, 1888–1923
      (4) Rufus M., 1891–1960
      (4) Jerry Lester, 1893–1961
      (4) Fate Grigsby, 1895–1951
      (4) Thelma, 1898–1982
      (4) Etta Ozelle, 1900–1982
      (4) John Tillman, 1903–1964, and Alma Altha Morris, 1907–1994
      (4) Guysell, 1905–199_
      (4) Buford Donald, 1908–1988
      (4) Thedford, 1910–1963

         (5) John Tillman, Jr., 1926–1990
         (5) Morris, 1928–2003
         (5) Alvin Newell, 1936–

Figure 2: Five Generations of Bellsburg Mitchells

CHAPTER 2

The Missing Mitchell

My father worked out much of the aforesaid by painstakingly tracking names and ages from one census to the next, fitting in names and dates from other records when available. The work involved many problems that continued to frustrate his attempts to go beyond William and Mary Mitchell.

One problem was the lack of census records for most of Tennessee before 1810. These records were destroyed during the War of 1812 when the British sacked Washington and burned the Library of Congress. Census records for several Virginia counties along the border with North Carolina were also burned. There were many Mitchells on both sides of the border, and many of them later turned up in Kentucky and Tennessee.

Another problem was William Mitchell's appearance in both Robertson and Dickson Counties. The Mitchell family seemed to move from Robertson County to Dickson County between 1820 and 1830, but, as my father figured later, they might also have stayed put while county boundaries changed. Before the creation of Cheatham County in 1856, Robertson County stretched clear across the Cumberland River between the mouth of the Harpeth and the juncture of Dickson and Montgomery Counties. An early map shows Dickson County fronting the Cumberland only at a point west of Palmyra, where Dickson, Montgomery, and Stewart Counties met. The land east of the Harpeth belonged to Davidson County, as did the mouth of the Harpeth on both sides. (The 1844 marriage of Aaron Pinson to Elizabeth Mitchell was recorded in Davidson County and likely took place at the settlement near the mouth of the Harpeth known then as Bellville.) Even today Cheatham County includes the mouth of the Harpeth on both sides from Pack Island to Dozier's Boat Dock (former site of Dozier's Restaurant). Cheatham also takes in a triangle of land south of the Cumberland between Dickson and Montgomery Counties. Thus, the Mitchell family would not have had to move to change counties if they had owned land near Bellsburg along the south bank of the Cumberland, where my father said the "Jack Mitchell bottom" lay.[8]

There is another reason for believing that the Mitchell family was living along the Cumberland in what is now Dickson County well before 1830. Land along the Cumberland was highly prized. It was flat, rich, well-watered, easily accessible, and consequently first to go in a land rush. In the 1820's, a humble farmer like William Mitchell could not have afforded to buy much Cumberland bottomland, and yet he owned enough of it to keep his sons and grandsons from having to migrate farther west for more land. He might have staked his claim on the land much earlier, and perhaps inherited it from his father or father-in-law, who might have received the land as a Revolutionary War land grant.

But who were his father and father-in-law? Mary Mitchell's maiden name is not known. My father guessed that it might have been Milton, as the couple's first son was named William Milton (remembered as "Uncle Milt"). There were Miltons in Sumner County north of Nashville, along the route into Middle Tennessee from Kentucky, but my father was never able to tie Mary to them. There were also Mitchells in Sumner County, one of which ran a tavern along the route into Tennessee, on whose land the town of Mitchellville was established in 1819. But again, my father was never able to tie William to them or to any other Mitchells in Dickson, Robertson, or Davidson Counties. The problem stumped him in 1986, and he did not return to it until late

---

[8] The "Jack Mitchell bottom" was the fertile, low-lying land Jack farmed, not the land on which he lived. The Cumberland Valley was prone to flooding, which was good for crops but destructive of homesteads. Jack would therefore have lived upland where Bellsburg is today, along the Harpeth Ridge, which runs between the Harpeth River and Johnson Creek.

1988, after spending time tracking down the Doziers, Morrises, Speights, and Frys.

Marriage records for Sumner County go back to 1786, but no marriage of William Mitchell to Mary Milton appears in them. William and Mary could have been married in Robertson County, where marriage records only go back to 1838. Yet on his second look, my father convinced himself that William Mitchell was not related to the other Mitchells of Robertson County. On January 25, 1989, he wrote:

> I have built a very, very strong case against any likelihood that my lineage goes through the 1820 Robertson Co. James Mitchell. The details of this may be found in my file labelled "Genealogy—Clues that went nowhere." However, in building this case, I was forced to reconsider some of the possibilities as to how and when my g. g. grandfather William got to Tennessee.

The problem with the Robertson County James was that he was married in Kentucky in 1787, four years before William Mitchell was born in North Carolina. (William's son Milt told census takers that his father was born in Tennessee, but Milt said the same about his mother Mary and was wrong. Mary twice told census takers that she was born in North Carolina, and her son Jack told the 1880 census taker that both his mother and his father were born in North Carolina.)

But William might have been born in North Carolina and then lived a while in Kentucky before moving to Tennessee. This opened up the possibility that William's father was George Mitchell who settled first in Kentucky, before turning up in Dickson County in 1806. The problem with George is that nothing ties him to William except a common last name. George is known to have had a son in Kentucky, named George Jr. Both Georges appear in the 1820 census, but nothing in the census ties them to William, who lived at the opposite end of the county. George Sr. was an early member of the Turnbull Primitive Baptist Church, in the southeast corner of the county; William Mitchell lived in the northeast corner (in another county originally), and his Mitchell descendants were Methodists. (Never mind that they were buried in a Presbyterian cemetery. Their Methodist church was farther away, so many Methodists in the Bellsburg area buried their kin instead at Mt. Liberty.)

It's the same with every other Dickson Mitchell. None lived near William or appear with him in county records. One Mitchell, first name unknown, kept a shop on the square in the county seat of Charlotte, which was a stop on the stagecoach route from Nashville to Jackson. Others Mitchells appear on land records for plots in Charlotte and along Yellow Creek, west of Charlotte. These early Dickson Mitchells knew each other, and some might have been brothers. A Thomas Mitchell sold a slave to a Samuel Mitchell in 1814 and served on a jury with a John Mitchell in 1815. Samuel and George were sometimes in court together as jurors. George appears many times in Dickson County records as a juryman and an appointee responsible for road maintenance, an indication that he owned property along the road from Nashville to Jackson.

William, on the other hand, was never called to serve on a jury or perform road maintenance. He rarely appears in the public records of Dickson County. He is counted by tax-collectors and census-takers as part of Robertson and then Dickson, and his daughter marries in Davidson. It seems that he spent his life on the river, between three counties, having little to do with the county in which he lived.

But even lacking evidence linking William to other Dickson County Mitchells, my father found it much more likely that William was related to some of the Mitchells in the area than that he was entirely on his own, without any kin nearby. George Sr. was not likely William's father, but the aforesaid Thomas, Samuel, and John could have been William's older brothers. The first Mitchell known to have settled in Dickson County was Thomas, who is mentioned in the histories as one of Dickson's earliest settlers, having arrived before 1804.

With nothing else to go on, my father turned again to North Carolina in search of a family that could have been William's, a family with a male child born about 1791 and older sons that could have been Thomas, John, or Samuel.

◆

In his early research, my father identified Granville County, North Carolina, as William Mitchell's likely birthplace. Granville is due north of Raleigh along the Virginia border. Mitchells had led the settlement

14

of that part of the country. In 1733, Colonel William Byrd II (1674–1744) wrote in his diary that, on a tour of the Virginia frontier, he had stayed the night at the settlement of one Peter Mitchell, whom he named "the highest Inhabitant of the Roanoke River," meaning that Peter lived farther up river than anyone else, on the very edge of the frontier. Byrd located Peter's settlement six miles from the confluence of the Roanoke and Dan Rivers. Even today, there is a Peter Creek running along the north bank of the Dan.

Peter Mitchell is easy to trace. There were only two in that part of the country at the time, and they were father and son. The elder Peter was "transported" to upper Surry County, Virginia, as an indentured servant by John Rawlins in 1692. He appeared with 305 acres on a roll for "quit rents" in neighboring Prince George County in 1704. In 1717, he bought land north of the Nottoway River, near the Prince George-Surry County line (now the Dinwiddie-Sussex County line). The next year, Peter Jr. bought land very nearby. In 1726, Peter Sr. of Prince George County bought land south of the Nottoway in Brunswick County, "opposite son Peter's plantation." Peter Jr. added to his "plantation" the next year, bringing his total acreage to 484. Peter Sr. then owned 458 acres on the Nottoway (not including the 305 acres he owned in 1704). A few years later, Peter Jr. moved farther inland to the Dan River, where Col. Byrd found him in 1733. This Peter bought another 242 acres on the north side of the Dan in 1741. His father died in 1739.

The progress of Peter Mitchell, *pere et fils*, is typical of nearly a dozen Mitchells in the area at the same time. The spelling of the name changes a few times (from *Michel* or *Michal*, to *Michell*, *Mitchel*, and finally *Mitchell*), but they appear to be all of one extended family. The fathers among them all arrived in Virginia as indentured servants, settled on the south side of the James River, and bought land farther inland and close to other Mitchells when they could. In 1723, there were nine Mitchells owning property on the Nottoway at the Prince George-Surry County line. They were Peter, Peter Jr., John, John Jr., Robert, Robert Jr., Henry, Henry Jr., and Thomas. (Only Edward Mitchell, who arrived in 1701, chose not to settle on the Nottoway at the Prince George-Surry County line; in the 1720's, he was buying land 15 miles northwest, on White Oak Creek.) Peter and John were the first to buy land on the Nottoway, both in 1717; the last Mitchell to appear in the area was James, in 1731. By that time, several of these Mitchells had already moved farther inland to the north bank of the Roanoke River. In the 1740's, some will move to the south bank of the Roanoke, and in the 1750's they will cross the state line into Granville County, North Carolina, to take advantage of a new offer of cheap land to encourage settlement. Then, after the Revolutionary War, their sons will cross the mountains, either through the Cumberland Gap into Central Kentucky or down the Clinch and Holston Rivers into East Tennessee and then on into Middle Tennessee by way of Avery's Trace, a wilderness road laid out in 1787 to connect the Knoxville area with Nashville.

The links from the Dan and Roanoke Rivers to the Cumberland and Harpeth Rivers are obvious and intriguing. Another family following the same path as the Mitchells were the Dukes. John Duke witnessed a sale of land on the Roanoke from Thomas Mitchell of Surry County to James Mitchell of Brunswick County in 1735, and David Mitchell and Robert Duke faced each other in court in Granville County in 1764. Then there is the appearance of Aaron Pinsons in both places. In *Early Settlers of Mecklenburg County, Virginia*, we read that "Aaron Pinson, Peter Mitchell, and William Hogan were the earliest settlers of record on the western boundary of the area now Mecklenburg County." In fact, the western boundary of what is now Mecklenburg County, Va., is Aarons Creek, which flows north from Granville County, N.C., into the Dan River, midway between Peters Creek to the west and the confluence of the Dan and the Roanoke to the east.

All of the aforesaid on the Mitchells of Virginia is the product of my own research, and it appears that my father knew little about them. He was intrigued by two other links between Granville County and the Cumberland Valley. One was the presence of two and possibly three generations of Tillmans in early Granville County: a John Tillman on Granville's tax list in 1755, 1769, and 1771; a George Tillman on Granville's tax list in 1769 and 1771; and the 1780 will of George Tillman naming sons William and John, daughter Elizabeth, and wife Polly.

The second and most intriguing link was the 1769 marriage of a young woman named Messenier Davis to one Abraham Mitchell in Granville County and the presence of an old woman named Missanier Mitchell in Montgomery County, Tenn., in 1820. My father suspected that this was William Mitchell's mother, and it appears from the records he pieced together that she very well could have been. These are the pieces:

(1) Messenier Davis, daughter of Solomon Davis, married Abraham Mitchell in Granville County in 1769.

(2) Thomas Henderson witnessed the marriage of Abraham and Messenier in 1769; Abraham Mitchell signed over rights to land in Kentucky in 1779 (when it was still of county of Virginia) to Samuel Henderson Jr., with Nathaniel Henderson as a witness.

(3) An Abraham Mitchell appears in the land records of Davidson County, Tenn., in 1793, when Davidson included what is now Dickson, Robertson, and Cheatham Counties (and much else).

(4) Messenah Mitchell appears in the 1800 census of Granville County as a woman over 45 who is the head of a household. Her age makes it possible for her to have been Abraham's bride: If Messenier Davis was 15 when she married, she would have been 46 in 1800.

(5) In Messenah's 1800 household are—
  -one male over 45 (possibly her invalid husband, but more likely her aged father)
  -one female 16 to 26
  -one male 10 to 16
  -one female 10 to 16
  -two males under 10 (one could have been William)
  -two females under 10

(6) Solomon Davis, 26–45, appears in the 1800 census of Granville County as the next listing after Messenah Mitchell. This must be Messenah's brother, as she herself is over 45.

(7) Solomon Davis's will, proved in February 1810, in Granville County, names his daughter Meseniah Mitchell and his under-age grandson Solomon Hunt. (His estate includes 40 negro slaves, some young, some old.)

(8) Mesniah Mitchell appears in the 1810 census of Granville County as a woman over 45 who is the head of a household with just one other female, 16 to 26.

(9) No Mesniah, Messenah, or Messenier Mitchell appears in any later census of Granville County.

(10) Missanier Mitchell appears in the 1820 census of Montgomery County, Tenn., as a woman over 45 and living alone.

(11) Mesnier Mitchell dies in 1823, and her will is probated in Clarksville. The court appoints Solomon Hunt (her now grown nephew, see 6 above) as an executor, with other executors who are not named in the records.

(12) No other Abraham Mitchell appears in North Carolina or Tennessee to match the Abraham who married Messenier in 1769 or the Abraham who claimed land in Davidson County in 1793.

Allowing for changes in the spelling of a very unusual name, one could easily construct a plausible account according to which Abraham Mitchell travels to Tennessee with his younger brothers, who are known to have served in the Revolutionary War, to establish claims on land in what was then Davidson County, then dies or disappears before he can move his family to Tennessee. (He would likely have been in his mid-40's in 1793 and might have fallen victim to illness or Indians.) His wife Messenier stays on in Granville County until her father dies in 1810 and her children are grown and gone. Then she follows her children to Tennessee, where her elder sons have settled Abraham's land. (The couple's grown sons could have accompanied Abraham to Tennessee in 1793 or arrived later to take up the claim.)

Missenier must have followed someone to Tennessee. Would she not have followed her own sons and daughters? We know that her nephew and executor Solomon Hunt was in the area when she died in 1823. (I have not checked census records for him.) We know also of two Mitchell families in Montgomery County in 1820. One was a large family of women and girls—eight females under 26—headed by a woman 26 to 45 named Delpha Mitchell, but this family is surely from Louisa County, Virginia, east of Charlottesville, where William Snelson Mitchell married Delpha Mallory in 1798. When Delphia Mitchell died in 1823, a court in Louisa County appointed Forest Hunter as guardian of the three female orphans of William S. Mitchell. This William could not have been our William's father because our William was born in North Carolina before William S. and Delpha were married in Virginia.

There was also a John Mitchell in Montgomery County in 1820. He was over 45 and living with a woman over 45 and a boy 10 to 16. This John must have been born before 1775. He could have been born as early as 1770 and still have been Missenier's son (she married in 1769). If he was born in 1770, he could have been William Mitchell's father, but he would have had to have been born close to 1770. If he was born as late as 1775, he would have still been in his teens when William and his older brother John Jr. were born between 1791 and 1794. It is possible that this John was both Missenier's son and William's father, but it is also possible that he is Missenier's son and William's older brother, for we know that Missenier still had three boys at home in 1800, and we can assume that she had other sons grown and gone by then, after 31 years of marriage.

John Mitchells appear only briefly in Robertson, Dickson, and Montgomery Counties in the early 1800's. A John Mitchell was declared insolvent in Montgomery County in 1808, most likely in the settlement of his estate *post mortem*. Two John Mitchells (and our William Mitchell) signed the 1812 Robertson County petition opposing the building of a jail in Springfield; one signed as "John Mitchell Sr." In 1815, a John Mitchell served on a jury with a William Mitchell in Robertson County, and a John Mitchell served on a jury with a Thomas Mitchell in Dickson County.

The Mitchells of Dickson County might not have lived very far from Missanier Mitchell in Montgomery County. The Jack Mitchell bottom is just six or seven miles upriver from the Montgomery County line, and Samuel Mitchell, who later lived in Dickson County, appears to have signed a Montgomery County petition in 1806 for separate elections in the settlement of Palmyra, which is down river from Clarksville on the south side of the Cumberland. There was also a "Mr. Mitchell" who joined two other partners in 1830 to operate the Mount Vernon furnace on Budds Creek just east of Palmyra on the south side of the Cumberland. This Mitchell is said to have retired from the partnership shortly thereafter. He could have been the John Mitchell in the 1820 census of Montgomery County, or he could have been Thomas or Samuel Mitchell of Dickson County. All three would have been the right age.

What seems certain is that Abraham Mitchell's widow and sons settled in Middle Tennessee between Clarksville and Nashville. His eldest son could have been 30 in 1800. This means that all of the early Dickson County Mitchells except the Turnbull Baptist George could have been Abraham and Missenier's children: Thomas, John, Samuel, and William.

◆

There were other suggested links between Granville County and Middle Tennessee that should be mentioned. There were David Mitchells in Granville before and after the Revolution, and there was a David Mitchell who signed the Cumberland Compact in 1780, as an original settler of Nashborough. There was a Daniel Mitchell who married Mary Gregg in Granville County in 1763, and a Daniel Mitchell who signed the Montgomery County petition for separate elections in the settlement of Palmyra in 1806, along with the aforesaid Samuel Mitchell. But in both cases, we have not enough evidence to say that the David or Daniel who appears in Granville County is or is not the David or Daniel who appears later in Middle Tennessee.

Some Mitchell families can be positively traced from North Carolina to Middle Tennessee, but none of these provides links to the Thomas, John, Samuel, or William Mitchell of Dickson County. Other Mitchell families in North Carolina had sons of the right ages to account for Thomas, Samuel, or William, but among these only the family of Abraham and Messenier provides a positive link to the lower Cumberland. Most of the other families can be traced to other parts of North Carolina or Tennessee.

This is what occupied my father's last months of genealogical research. In the end, he was left with two or three possibilities and a lot of loose ends—Mitchells who can't be traced anywhere. Unable to say which Mitchells were our William's parents, my father then turned to sorting out the relationships of the possibilities to each other. His last notes were dated March 3, 1989.[9] They record the names in the wills of several North Carolina Mitchells in the 1700's.

◆

---

[9] My father, John Tillman Mitchell Jr., died of cancer in July of 1990, just before his 64th birthday.

When I began my own research while in Houston in the mid 1990's, I started where my father left off, working backward from the wills to find out more about the Mitchells of Granville County, but I did so with different aims and interests. My father's chief interest in genealogy was the challenge of solving a mystery; his aim was always to established each link in the lineage with utmost certainty. He would not presume links that could not be proved or let his research run too far afield of the problem of proof. My interest in genealogy was more historical and cultural; my aim was to understand the origins of the culture I have inherited. It therefore mattered less to me that I could not say for certain who William Mitchell's parents were, if it seemed likely that they came from a certain set of Mitchells.

Fortunately for me, the available evidence seems to show that the remaining possibilities and the many loose ends come from the same set of Mitchells. Several were quite closely related: The Daniel Mitchell who married Mary Gregg in 1763 was likely the son of Robert Mitchell, who was the brother-in-law of James Mitchell, who was the father of Abraham Mitchell, who was the brother of David Mitchell, who was the father of Elijah Mitchell, who had several sons who could have been Thomas, Samuel, and William Mitchell of Dickson County (though Elijah himself is known to have stayed in Granville County until 1810).

With these Mitchells, we can go back at least a generation further: James, the father of Abraham, was the son of John Mitchell of Lunenburg County, Virginia, who died in 1753 leaving his land and slaves to his grandson and namesake John, youngest child of James' widowed sister Catherine, whose husband Robert Mitchell died in 1751. Robert and Catherine had five children older than John, including sons Robert, Isaac, and Daniel. Son Isaac was named after James's and Catherine's brother Isaac, a common practice in those days. Son Daniel might have been named after an older Daniel Mitchell who in 1748 paid tithes to Cumberland Parish in Lunenburg County, Virginia, which was then across the state line from Granville County. Son Robert shows up on a 1754 muster roll of the North Carolina militia in the French and Indian War. His company commander was Capt. John Glover. He later married Susannah Glover, and his brother Isaac married Phoebe Glover.

That this younger Robert was already of enlistment age in 1754 means that his grandfather John was likely in his 60's when he died in 1753. If he was in his late 60's, he could have been the John Mitchell who paid "quit rents" in Prince George County, Virginia, in 1704, and also the John Mitchell who was transported to Isle of Wight County, Virginia, as an indentured servant in 1698. (Both counties are on the south side of the James River.) The advanced age of the John who died in 1753 weighs in favor of his being one or both of the earlier Johns, over another John Mitchell who died in 1745 in Brunswick County, Virginia. This other John left his wife Judy, son William, daughter Kersia, daughter Sukie, and son John, but no clues as to how old he was at death. (His executors were James and William Maclin. There is still today a Maclins Creek north of Emporia, Virginia, in what was then Brunswick County. The creek is about ten miles due south of the spot on the Nottoway where the Mitchells congregated in the 1720's and 1730's. Ten miles due south of Maclins Creek is the crossroad of Mitchells Mill, just off Interstate 95 at the first exit north of the state line.)

◆

The Mitchell about whom the most is known is Abraham's father James. This James Mitchell was a leading citizen in the new county of Lunenburg, separated from Brunswick County in 1746. James and three other "gentlemen" were appointed to scout out a good location for Lunenburg County's seat, but the site they chose was criticized as unsuitable, and a new site was selected. From 1746 to 1752, James served as justice of the county court, and in 1753 he was the county sheriff. That year, however, he failed to account for 34,865 pounds of tobacco collected as tax and was later convicted of making false returns.

By that time, James already owned large tracts of land in both Virginia and North Carolina. He appears to have bought his first plot of land in 1731, at the gathering of Mitchells on the Nottoway, where his father John had owned land since 1722. Then in 1735 James followed Thomas, Peter Jr., and John Jr. to the Roanoke, where he first bought 250 acres on the north bank from Thomas, who had settled there in 1728. The next year James expanded his holdings with the purchase of three more tracts south of the Roanoke near the state line. James was among the first in Virginia to receive land grants in Granville County, N.C., in 1751. Land records for 1751 style him "Captain James Mitchell," no doubt his former rank in the Virginia militia. Captain James bought more land in Granville in 1754, but he continued to live in Virginia. A map of early settlements in Granville County shows James's homestead just north of the state line.

Later on, James began selling off his holdings in Virginia. In 1759, he sold 829 acres in Lunenburg County to Edmund Taylor, with David Mitchell as a witness. Then in 1767, James's wife Amy sold to Colonel Edmund Taylor 2,226 acres in Mecklenburg County, which had been created out of the southern half of Lunenburg County in 1765.

James died in Granville County in 1777. His will named sons Josiah, David, John, and Abraham; daughters Amy Satterwhite and Mary Bullock; grandson Randol and granddaughter Elizabeth. His wife Amy is not named and likely died before he did. Another son named James also is not named in the will. He is likely the James Mitchell who served as an ensign in Captain John Sallis's company from Granville County during the French and Indian War. He appears in county tax lists with "James Sr." in 1769 and 1771, but not thereafter. We can assume that he, too, died before his father.

James's sons Josiah and David also served in the French and Indian War, but in separate companies. Josiah served alongside Robert Mitchell in Captain Glover's company. David served alongside brother James Jr. in Captain Sallis's company. Josiah appears regularly in Granville County tax lists from 1755 to 1790. David appears in Granville County tax lists from 1769 to 1790. He is said to have owned the Belvidere Plantation northeast of Henderson, N.C., which was then in Granville County. When he died in 1790, his plantation went to his eldest son Elijah, who was still in Granville in 1810. It is therefore not likely that James's son David was the David Mitchell who made the trek to Tennessee with James Robertson and signed the Cumberland Compact in 1780 and who appears on Davidson County tax records in 1793. James's son John also remained in Granville County, where the federal census of 1800 shows him owning 28 slaves.

James's youngest son Abraham was too young to serve in the French and Indian War and too old to serve in the Revolutionary War. He appears on the Granville tax lists in 1771 and 1784. As mentioned above, he may be the Abraham Mitchell in the tax list for Davidson County, Tennessee, in 1793, though his wife is known to have stayed in Granville County until after 1810.

CHAPTER 3

English, Scottish, Irish, or Scotch-Irish?

Now to answer the question that most interested me: Who were these Mitchells who settled south of the James River, moved inland into North Carolina, and then crossed the mountains into Middle Tennessee? Were they Scottish, Irish, Scotch-Irish, English, or Welsh?

Grady Mitchell told my father that his father had told him they were Scotch-Irish, but this is a common assumption among Southerners that is often based more on an ethnic myth of the mid–1800's than on real knowledge of our roots. The myth claimed Scottish heritage for the descendants of settlers from Ulster Ireland, who had thereto called themselves Irish.[10] "Scotch-Irish" is an Americanism meant to distinguish these early settlers from the Irish Catholic immigrants who came much later, many of them fleeing the Great Potato Famine (1845–1852). It also served to associate the new Southern aristocracy of Jacksons, Polks, and Calhouns with the romance of Scotland popularized in the mid–1800's by Sir Walter Scott. (Scott's *Ivanhoe* was a best-selling novel in the antebellum South.) More recently, conservative Southerners have modified the Scotch-Irish myth to claim "Celtic" heritage, distinct from the anti-traditional Anglo-Saxon heritage of the Yankee elite. But like all ethnic myths, this one takes great liberties with the historical reality.

---

[10] Ulster is the one of the four ancient provinces of Ireland (the others being Leinster, Munster, and Connaught). Six of its nine counties are now the country of Northern Ireland, which is part of the United Kingdom and not part of the Republic of Ireland.

To begin with, early Americans who were identifiably Irish or Scottish were always a minority in the American states. One study puts the share of Scottish and Irish surnames in the 1790 census at 32.3 percent in North Carolina and 35.3 percent in Tennessee. Another study puts the same share at 40.9 percent in North Carolina (no estimate for Tennessee). South Carolina had the most, with 36.5 percent in the first study and 44.6 percent in the second. The remainder in all of the states was mostly English and Welsh. Goodspeed's 1887 *History of Cheatham County* confirms this. The chapter on Cheatham County includes brief biographies of fifty or so long-time residents, making 37 claims of specific European ancestry, as follows:

English	13
Irish	6
German	5
Scotch-Irish	4
Welsh	3
Scotch	3
French	2
Swiss	1

No doubt, several of those claiming Irish or "Scotch" ancestry are what we would today call Scotch-Irish, but when we add them up we find that just 35 percent of the population of Cheatham County claimed Irish, Scottish, or Scotch-Irish descent, while 43 percent claimed English or Welsh descent. (One who claimed English and French descent was Enoch Dozier, nephew of my great-great-great-grandfather Grandie E. Dozier.)

Let us not forget that the colonies had seen a hundred years of settlement from England before the great migrations from Ulster in the 1700's. In Virginia's first hundred years, three out of four settlers came as indentured servants, and most of those came from southern England, shipping out of London or Bristol. Closer to 1700, the source of indentured servants shifted northward to England's North Country, the Scottish Lowlands, and Ulster. The first great migration of families from Ulster did not begin until 1717–1718, but the Ulster Irish themselves were a mix of Irish aboriginals, Lowland Scots, and English settlers. The English predominated in the Ulster counties of Armagh and Derry. The land around Belfast in County Antrim was settled by Englishmen from Devon in southwest England and from Lancashire and Cheshire on England's northwest coast.

This mix of British peoples can be seen in the servants transported to Virginia's Isle of Wight County on the south side of the James River by one John Giles in 1698. They were:

James Tullagh
James Tullagh Jr.
Jacob Price
David Surry
Michael Conway
Samuel Leach
Thomas Catch
John Mitchell

We do not know where these men came from, but their surnames give us clues. *Tullagh* is an Irish toponym (place name). *Surry* is an English toponym (for someone from the southern county of Surrey). *Conway* (or *Conwy*) is a Welsh toponym but also an English spelling of several similar-sounding Irish names. *Price* is either a Welsh patronym (from *ap Rhys*, or son of Rhys) or an English metonym (occupational name) for a fixer of prices. *Catch* is an English metonym for a catcher of game. *Leach* is an English metonym for a physician from the Old English word for physician (not because they used leeches to drain the body of blood, but because prehistoric healers presumed to heal by incantation).

Mitchell, the most common of the eight names, is most often a patronym for *Michael*, which was commonly pronounced *Mitchell* in the Middle Ages and often spelled *Michel* up until the 1800s. The name was widespread even many years ago. There was a Gilbert Michel in the northern county of Northumberland in 1205, and a Robert Michel in the southern county of Somerset in 1219. There was also in 1219 a William Michel who was paid for keeping the king's wolfhounds in Middleton, Wiltshire. He is believed to be the son of Michael de Middleton, who kept the king's wolf-hounds in 1198. *Mitchell* can also come from an English nickname meaning "the big" (related to the word *much*, as in Ralph le Muchele from 1230). Mitchells of this origin appear early in Wiltshire, Somerset, and Essex, all in the south of England. But most *Mitchell* surnames originated as patronyms, as surnames originating as nicknames are relatively rare.

Noticeably absent from the list above are any distinctively Scottish names, though it would not have been unusual to find English names in the Scottish Lowlands, where much of the population was of mixed ancestry, the result of English domination of the Lowlands beginning in the seventh century. As noted in the introduction, *Mitchell* is today among the twenty most common names in Scotland. *David* was also a popular first name in Scotland and in Scottish Ulster, but it was even more popular in Wales because the patron saint of Wales was a St. David of Mynyw in Pembrokeshire (+589). *Davis* and *Davies* are common Welsh patronyms. As for the other first names, *Jacob* suggests Presbyterian Protestantism, the dominant faith of the Scotch-Irish. *Michael* combined with *Conway* sounds Irish Catholic, and, coincidentally, there were Irish Conways going back several centuries in southwest Ireland's County Clare, where there is also today a Tullagh (or Tulla) parish. Otherwise, the first names are too common to tell us much.

All things considered, it seems unlikely these eight men were recruited from Scotland or from the more Scottish counties of Ulster. Dublin in Leinster or Liverpool ("Dublin's Backyard") in England are more likely. The names hardly qualify as Scotch-Irish; they are rather a mix of English and Irish, which we also find in northwest England. Some modern historians prefer the more general term "North Britons," which includes the truly Scotch-Irish with the Anglo-Irish of Ulster, English and Scottish borderers, and other English Northerners. Altogether these people did constitute the dominant ethnicity of the American frontier from the early 1700's onward.

The evidence of this is hard to miss in Tennessee. Cumberland is an English county on the Scottish border. The Rutherfords, Hendersons, and Bells were border clans that made their living "reaving," "rustling," and "raiding." (The word *raid* is a border version of *road*, both derived from the verb *ride*.) Alvin York's ancestors came from York, and Cordell Hull's came from Hull in Yorkshire. James

Robertson, Nashville's founding father, is also reputed to have descended from a Yorkshire family whose name was originally *Robinson*. Many of the surnames common in Dickson and Cheatham Counties are also from Yorkshire: *Speight* is a Yorkshire word for woodpecker; *Duke* is often short for Marmaduke, a distinctively Yorkshire name; *Tidwell* comes from Tideswell, a village in Derbyshire, the next county south from Yorkshire; *Hudson* and *Dodson* (on my mother's side) are both Yorkshire names. The latter is sometimes spelled *Dodgson* in Yorkshire and shortened to *Dodds* on the border in Northumberland.

But what about the Granville Mitchells? We cannot know for sure that the Granville Mitchells descend from the John Mitchell transported by John Giles in 1698, but we do know that they descend from the Mitchells who settled south of the James River in the early 1700's and congregated on the Nottoway River in the 1720's. They did not arrive with the great migrations of Scotch-Irish to the Pennsylvania backcountry beginning in 1717. Those Scotch-Irish moved south into the Shenandoah Valley in 1730, then eastward into central Virginia in the 1740's, finally reaching the Carolina Piedmont, just west of Granville County, in the 1750's. No, the Granville Mitchells were already on the lower Roanoke River in 1728 and were buying land south of the Roanoke along the North Carolina border in 1736.

We also know the first names of these Mitchells, and they are telling. The Mitchells who congregated on the Nottoway were Peter, Peter Jr., John, John Jr., Robert, Robert Jr., Henry, Henry Jr., Thomas, and James. There was also an Edward Mitchell not far away. These are all common English names, but they are not all common Irish or Scottish names: *Edward* and *Robert* were too English for the truly Irish, and *Peter* was too papist for Scottish Presbyterians, who were also not particularly fond of the unbiblical *Henry* (perhaps on account of Henry VIII's "Rough Wooing" of Scotland in the early 1500's). Notice also that in these first two generations of Mitchells there were no distinctively Scotch-Irish names like *Patrick*, *Andrew*, *Alexander*, or *David*. *David* appears in the third generation, but *Patrick*, *Andrew*, and *Alexander* do not appear in the records of Granville County Mitchells until the 1800's. (They do not appear among my Mitchells until my own generation, and then only as middle names.)

I am therefore inclined to believe that these Mitchells are of English ancestry, most likely from England's North Country, possibly by way of Ulster, but still English and not Scottish, Irish, or Scotch-Irish.

Whether we are descended from them is still to be proved. It would help if we knew the contents of Missanier Mitchell's 1823 will, which might still be in the Montgomery County archives.

Modern science might provide other clues. I have recently made contact with a circle of Mitchells (some from Sumner Co., Tenn.) who claim or suspect their descent from the Granville Co. Mitchells. These people have begun DNA testing and so far have identified two distinct groups, one arguably descended from a Nimrod Mitchell, who appears but briefly in Granville Co., and the other arguably descended from the Henry Mitchells of Prince George Co., Va., the same Henry Mitchells who lived along the Nottoway. I have not yet submitted my DNA sample (the fee is $171), but will someday soon.

This ends my summary of findings completed in 2003.
What follows was written in 2021 and 2022.

CHAPTER 4

What a Difference a DNA Makes

I never got around to taking the DNA test mentioned at the end the preceding chapter. Besides the cost, I heard from one of the takers of the test that it had failed to connect her own brother with the rest of the family. This was in 2003, in early days of commercial DNA testing, so I figured I would wait for the science and the industry to develop before giving it a try.

The first DNA test I paid for was not for me but for my younger daughter, Paula, when she was in high school. In preparing college applications, she was asked repeatedly about her ethnicity, and going to a very multicultural high school with a lot of other brown-haired, brown-eyed people from other parts of the world, she thought that maybe she could claim Hispanic or Native American descent, or maybe something even more exotic. So, for her birthday I gave her a DNA kit, and she sent it off. The results were hardly surprising: In order of greatest to least, she was, like a lot of Americans, a mix of Scottish, British, and Northwestern European, with a slight trace of Mediterranean and no trace at all of anything Indian, African, or Asian. (These results, of course, included her mother's contribution, and her mother is known to have Scottish, English, and Dutch ancestry.)

The imprecision of the results did not make me think much of DNA testing for genealogical purposes. But then, in the insane summer of 2020, a Larry Mitchell in Michigan wrote to a Don Mitchell in Nashville asking him to take a particular DNA test for men that uses 111 genetic markers of their Y chromosome to identify those men who probably share a common male ancestor. Larry had sent the same request to many other Mitchell men in the hope of linking them to the same colonial forefather. He didn't know Don personally; he only knew that someone online had claimed that Don was descended from a William Mitchell who immigrated to Virginia in 1655 and whose descendants lived in Virginia's Lancaster and Richmond Counties before migrating to Robertson County, Tennessee, after the Revolutionary War. Don's full name is Buford Donald Mitchell Jr., and his father Buford was my father's uncle, making Don my father's first cousin and my first cousin once removed, "once removed" meaning one generation of difference, as shown here:

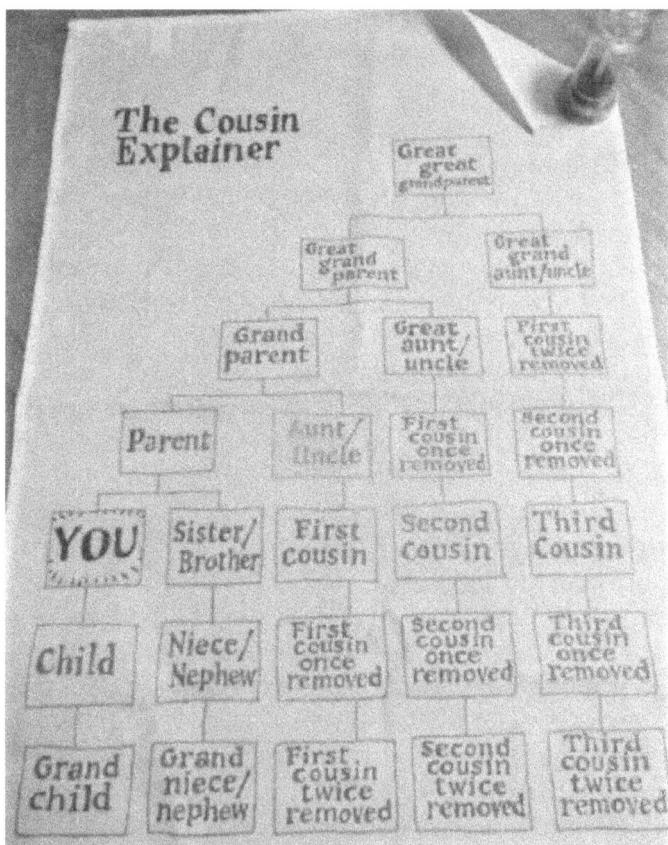

Figure 3

As one of the few surviving Mitchells of my father's generation, Don had already heard from my sister Dianne, who had begun researching genealogy in an attempt at membership in the Daughters of the American Revolution (DAR). The DAR is extremely demanding of official proof of descent, and it took her years to satisfy them (by descent from **Ralph Hoard Smith**, see pp. 65 and 68). In her attempt, she contacted Don, who later passed on Larry's request to her, who then passed it on to me.

I emailed Larry to find out what he knew or suspected about our relation, doubting his connection of Robertson County Mitchells to Lancaster and Richmond County Mitchells. Just as I expected, he didn't have any evidence to support the connection other than a John Mitchell here and then a John Mitchell there, about the same age and therefore assumed to be the same. But I took his requested yDNA test from FamilyTreeDNA, and, lo, it turned out that Larry and I are indeed *not* related, at least not in the male line.

It did, however, identify two other Mitchells, both of Robertson County, to whom I am related. One was Robert Wayne "Bob" Mitchell, a retired Army colonel who flew Hueys in Vietnam and spent his last years tracking his genealogy but who died in 2015. The other was James C. Mitchell, who knew Bob and still had access to Bob's private Ancestry.com pages. Both Bob and James were both descendants of John Mitchell Sr. and John Mitchell Jr. of Robertson County, who now appear to be the father and brother of my thrice-great-grandfather, William Mitchell, father of Jack Mitchell. That would make Bob and James my fifth cousins.

The evidence for these relations extends beyond the yDNA connecting me to Bob and James to include official records collected by Bob and shared with me by James. My father knew of the two Robertson County John Mitchells, Sr. and Jr., but the only evidence known to my father of a connection between them and our William was the 1812 petition opposing the building of a jail in Springfield, which was signed by a William Mitchell, a John Mitchell, and a John Mitchell Sr. To that fact on record, Bob Mitchell added these:

1.   In October 1815, **John Mitchell Sr.** sold to Samuel Murphey 89 acres on Calebs Creek, five miles west of Springfield. The record

of sale noted that John had purchased this land in 1808. **William Mitchell** witnessed the sale, which was registered by the county in March 1816.

2. In June 1816, **John Mitchell Sr.** bought 100 acres along Calebs Creek from William Gilbert and Nancy Price; **John Mitchell Jr.** (and Zacharias Duncan) witnessed the sale.

3. In October 1816, **John Mitchell** [Sr. or Jr.] bought from George Murphy 38 acres on which "John Mitchell now lives." **William Mitchell** (and Jeremiah Morris) witnessed the sale, which was proven in court in May 1817.

4. In 1823, **William Mitchell** and others were appointed by the Robertson County court to "lay off dower" for Mary Saunders, widow of Andrew Saunders, meaning they were to decide which acres of the deceased husband's land were to be retained by his widow.

5. In 1824, Thomas Williams deeded to **William Mitchell** 125 acres three miles north of Cheap Hill (now in Cheatham County), including the headwaters of Sugar Fork of Spring Creek, just off the road leading down to Weakley's Ferry, which crossed the Cumberland near the mouth of the Harpeth. There's a pretty little farm on William's land today, set back from the road a bit, about 11 miles southwest of Caleb's Creek, where John Sr. and John Jr. lived.

With these facts on record, plus yDNA, it now seems that our William Mitchell was the son of John Mitchell Sr. of Robertson County. We also now have no reason to speculate on how William's movement from Robertson County to Dickson County might just have been a change of county boundaries. William did certainly live in Robertson County, and he did certainly move across the Cumberland sometime after his 1824 purchase of land near Cheap Hill and before the 1830 census, which found him, his wife, and all their children in the Bellsburg area of Dickson County.

The move to Bellsburg is also supported by Robertson County Mitchell lore, as handed down by the Reverend George Franklin Mitchell to W. Ray Walker, who handed it down to me. Rev. Mitchell was born in 1869 and died 1970 at the age of 101. According to Ray, Rev. Mitchell was the great-great-grandson of John Mitchell Sr.

through his elder son, John Jr., brother of William. He was also Ray Walker's great uncle. Ray was born in 1926, the same year as my father, and is today 95 years old. He never knew his grandfathers, so he turned to Uncle George to find out more about the Mitchells of Robertson County. One day while driving around the countryside and pointing out where all the old homeplaces once were, George told Ray that "Bill" (my third great-grandfather William) had left Cheap Hill and moved to Bellsburg and was the father of all the Mitchells in that part of Dickson County.

So, the story of William's move to Dickson County in the 1820's was told to a young George in the 1870's, then told by George to Ray in the 1960's, then told by Ray to me in 2021. It seems I have received this 190-year-old story third-hand, with just three people between me and the move: Ray, George, and George's father or grandfather, who witnessed the move. (To have this happen in my family, my great-grandfather Ben West would have had to live to 1962, instead of dying in 1916, and my father would have to be alive today, instead of dying in 1990.)

◆

Many other things are claimed online about John Sr. and his son William. It is said that William's wife was named Mary Margaret Stewart. It is said that John Sr.'s wife was named Tabitha; it is also said that his wife was named Elizabeth Ann Hardwick. It is said that the Robertson County James Mitchell (known to my father and discounted by him as William's father) was John Sr.'s brother; that their father's name was also James and that this James died in Richmond County on Virginia's Northern Neck, the peninsula of land between the Potomac and Rappahannock Rivers[11]; that this James's father and grandfather were both named William, the latter of which died in Accomack County on Virginia's Eastern Shore in 1685; and that their lineage has been traced all the way back to England, where there is still a fine old ancestral home of the Mitchell clan.

Some of the foregoing may be true. There was in fact a James Mitchell among the early settlers of Robertson County, living in the

---

[11] Virginia's Richmond County was formed in 1692 and is 40 miles northeast of the city of Richmond, incorporated in 1742.

northwest corner of the county along Elk Fork Creek, which crosses over into Kentucky. And there was an Andrew Stewart who lived just west of Cheap Hill along Half Pone Creek; we know this because the county charged him with maintaining the road crossing the creek and leading down to another ferry. This Stewart was born in 1776 to John and Mary Stewart, according to Goodspeed's 1887 *History of Cheatham County*. In 1821, he married Margaret Morris, daughter of Jeremiah and Elizabeth Morris from North Carolina. As noted above, Jeremiah Morris joined William Mitchell in witnessing John Mitchell's purchase of property from George Murphy in 1817. So William knew Jeremiah and very likely knew Andrew and could have married Andrew's sister or another daughter of Jeremiah. After all, William's wife Mary was also born in North Carolina, as was Margaret Morris. But none of these facts supports Mary's maiden name being Mary Margaret Stewart. She seems to have been confused with Andrew's much younger daughter named Mary, who might indeed have been named Mary Margaret after his mother and his wife.

Evidence is thin to nonexistent for most everything else alleged online about the ancestry of William's father, John Sr., and my own interest in such allegations is limited by both the lack of evidence connecting William and John Sr. to earlier Mitchells and the strength of yDNA evidence connecting them to other early settlers not named Mitchell.

To date, over 600 men surnamed Mitchell have taken one of FamilyTreeDNA's several tests of yDNA. The fact that just two have been matched to me (my fifth cousins Bob and James) and that those two both descend from John Mitchell Sr. of Robertson County would seem to indicate that the Mitchell name entered our paternal line by what is called a "non-paternity event" such as (in order of frequency) illegitimacy, adoption, pseudonymity, or, in the present day, court order (a legal name change for reasons other than adoption).

Bob and James were not the only men matched to me by FamilyTreeDNA; 45 other men were, of which 28 are surnamed Ralston, Rolston, Rollston, Raulston, Roulston, Roulstone, or Rolleston (including 17 of the 22 who took the test I took for 111 genetic markers). The remaining 17 are a mix of unrelated names: Absten, Alston, Baxter, Dickerson, Gardner, Eatherton, Moote, Southard, Young, and

Yule. Some of these 17 are known to have been adopted and bear the surname of their adopting father. Besides the two Mitchells, the closest yDNA match are named Charles G. Absten and Don G. Baxter. Baxter (1932–2017) was from Colorado and Kansas and claimed descent from a John Baxter who was born in Scotland in 1727. Absten is from West Virginia and has very recently tested his yDNA. Nothing else is known about his ancestry at this time.

Except for yDNA, there is no known connection between the Mitchells and the other matches. There was a David Ralston who settled west of Goodlettsville, on Whites Creek in Davidson County, Tenn., in 1787. His log cabin is still there, in fine shape, with a large modern addition, at 5321 Lickton Pike. I was sent a recent photo of it by Ed Ralston, David Ralston's fifth-great-grandson and an administrator of the Ralston Project, a genealogical collaboration of descendants linked by FamilyTreeDNA. David's cabin is about 20 miles southeast of where John Sr. lived on Calebs Creek in Robertson County, which might suggest close kinship between John and David, but Ed, who has looked long and hard at this possibility, is convinced their living so close was coincidental.[12] Nothing else known about John or David links them together, and there were other Ralstons living much closer to Mitchells a generation earlier in Virginia. For much of the past year, theses Ralstons were the focus of my research.

In the shadow of Virginia's Blue Ridge Mountains, along the present path of Interstate 81, six miles south of the James River and ten miles north of Roanoke, in what was then Augusta County and is now Botetourt County, there once lived a William Ralston.[13] Some believe this William was born in Boston as the son of a John Raulston of a family of Scottish merchants, but others dismiss this Boston

---

[12] For more about David Ralston, including photos of his cabin near Goodlettsville, visit https://davidralston.info.

[13] Botetourt (pronounced "BOT-a-tot") was the first county formed from Augusta County, in 1770. Rockingham (centered on Harrisonburg) and Rockbridge (centered on Lexington) were created from Augusta in 1791, with the former north and the latter south of what remained of Augusta (centered on Staunton). Botetourt (centered on tiny Fincastle) remains the most rural of the four since the creation of Roanoke County from Botetourt in 1838.

connection as unsupported by evidence and contrary to historical patterns of migration. William died in 1767, but he left behind six or seven sons: Robert, John, David, William, Samuel, Matthew, and Andrew, all believed to have been born between 1728 and 1745. Most of the seven started out living 70 to 80 miles north of Botetourt County, in the vicinity of Harrisonburg, before the Revolutionary War, but John is known to have settled along Looney's Mill Creek, a tributary of the James, as early as 1751, and just two years later his father, William Sr., is known to have settled right about where Looney's Mill Creek begins, 10 miles southwest of the James, near the tiny settlement of Trinity, which appears just above "Wm. Ralston" in the upper right corner of this map of early plantations in what was once the Greenfield-Amsterdam Community of Botetourt County:

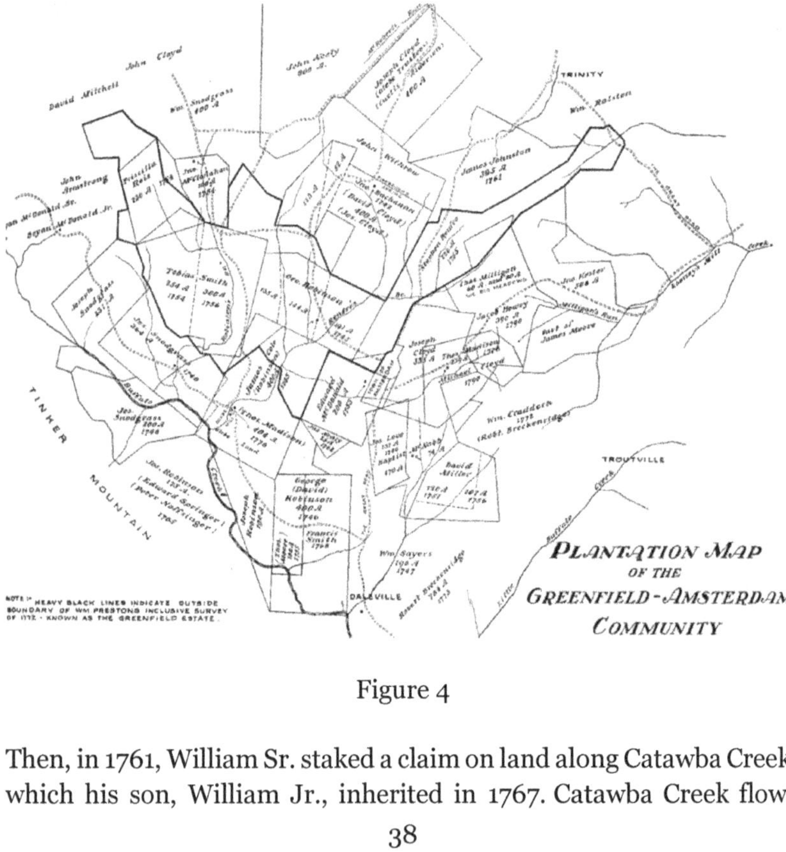

Figure 4

Then, in 1761, William Sr. staked a claim on land along Catawba Creek, which his son, William Jr., inherited in 1767. Catawba Creek flows northeast into the James just off the upper left corner of the map above, and, lo, in that corner we also find "David Mitchell."

This David Mitchell appeared in court in Orange County, Virginia, on February 28, 1739, to swear an Oath of Importation entitling him to "headrights" to unsettled land in the grant of William Beverley (1696–1756) in newly created Augusta County west of the Blue Ridge Mountains.[14] To encouragement settlement, headrights were offered to males 16 or older who swore in court that they had transported themselves from Great Britain at their own expense and not as indentured servants. Their Oaths of Importation often recorded their place of origin and port of entry. In David's case, the court noted only that "David Mitchell made oath that he imported himself, Martha, Sarah, James & Eliza Mitchell at his own Charge into the Colony and that this is the first time of proving his or their rights to Land."

Not noted by the court is that the Martha whom David imported was not his wife but his widowed mother, for in October of the same year, "Martha Mitchell of Orange County, widow," was granted 279 acres two miles due north of David's land in Augusta County between Staunton and Lexington, near the town of Greenville. His land and her grant are both easily visible in the southwest section of a map of the Beverley Patent produced in 1954 by J.R. Hildebrand.[15]

Martha's will of 1758 confirms that she had two sons, David and James, of which the court noted:

> As her son David Mitchell, through the necessity of the times, hath been forced to leave his own habitation, he is to live with James until it pleases God to restore peace to the land. Executors, David and James Mitchell, her sons.

---

[14] Augusta County was created from Orange County in 1738, but it was not provided with its own courts until 1745, before which settlers of Augusta had to travel to Orange to appear in court.

[15] See http://www.usgenwebsites.org/vagenweb/augusta/BeverlyPatent.html. The Eleanor and John Mitchell in the same corner of the map are another widow and son who may or may not be related to David and Martha, as will be explained in the next chapter.

The "necessity of the times" refers to the French and Indian War (1754–1763), during which settlers in the Upper Valley, southwest of Beverley Manor, fell victim to Indian raids.[16]

David and James did not stay in Beverley Manor. Between 1742 and 1744, David acquired over 1,100 acres south of the James River, 40 miles southwest of Beverley Manor, including 660 acres on Catawba Creek. This made him neighbors of first William Ralston Sr. and then William Ralston Jr. His brother James also bought land in the area, at Fork Bottom, where Catawba Creek and Lapsley Run meet the James, but he bought it in 1753 and was prevented from settling there permanently by the French and Indian War. He sold that property after the war but was again buying property in the area in 1784 to give his sons, Samuel and Edward, in 1786 and 1787. A few years later, he and his sons moved to Kentucky.

David also returned to Catawba Creek after the war, where he built a water grist mill in 1768, which he operated for many years. He was very often in court as either plaintiff or defendant, usually to settle business disputes. He appears on Botetourt County's personal property tax list for 1784, owning 596 acres at the time, but just three cows, two horses, and no slaves. Nothing is known of his wife or children, but he was not entirely alone in 1785, when the county recorded one other white person living with him or in one of the three other

---

[16] While exploring the frontier in 1755, William Beverley's land agent James Patton was murdered by Shawnee Indians in the Draper's Meadow Massacre near present-day Blacksburg, Virginia. Four other settlers were also murdered, including an infant whose brains were bashed out against the logs of a cabin. Two young women were captured by the Indians and taken to Ohio, but they escaped and returned to Virginia to tell the story. William Preston, whose name also appears on the map on page 38, was with Patton but left the party before the massacre and survived. Patton had served in the Royal Navy and owned his own ship, which he sailed from Ulster to Virginia 25 times bringing colonists destined for Beverley Manor. The colonists disembarked at Tappahannock on the Rappahannock River and proceeded westward by land through Orange County, which bordered Augusta County when the latter was created in 1738. The other major route into the Shenandoah Valley was from the north, through Philadelphia and Lancaster County, Pennsylvania, then through western Maryland.

dwellings he then owned.[17] Yet when he died in 1787, he left no will designating heirs, and his brother James was forced to sue their two sisters and brothers-in-law for a share of David's remaining 620 acres; the court divided the land roughly three ways in 1796, giving James 200 acres with David's "old habitation."

◆

The main limitation in our knowledge of David and James Mitchell is that it leaves us without a woman of the same generation as William Ralston Sr.'s sons. This is not unusual for the time. Women rarely attracted official notice except as owners of property or heirs named in wills. Children born out of wedlock received even less notice. Augusta County court records between 1745 and 1800 name just two (one because he was murdered by his mother).

There was, however, one quite curious court case in early Augusta County involving not just a Mitchell woman but a Mitchell mother and her son. On page 441 of volume 1 of Lyman Chalkley's 1912 extracts of Augusta County court records, we find this very odd note:

> Examination of Margaret Mitchell, wife of William Mitchell, and daughter of Ephraim McDowell, 1753. She had a son.

The birth of sons to mothers was not normally the business of county courts in those days. Why was it in this case? Why would a mother need to be examined by the court, unless the paternity of her son were in doubt? Why would her father be named by the court along with her husband, unless her reputation were at issue? And why was her son not identified as William Mitchell's? Margaret definitely appears to have had a reputation. A few years earlier, in 1749, she and her husband William were sued for slander by neighbors named David and Mary Moore.

We know a little more about her father, Ephraim McDowell, who had emigrated from Ulster, where, at 16, he fought among the

---

[17] All of David's land was by grant and not purchase. One staked a claim and then obtained a patent granting rights to the claim. One way of staking a claim was to build a cabin, establishing "cabin rights" to the land. This would explain David's four dwellings.

Protestant "Defenders of Derry" against the Irish Catholic army of the deposed English king James II at the Siege of 1689 and at the Battle of the Boyne in 1690. Some say Ephraim sailed to America in 1729 aboard the infamous *George and Ann* or its sister ship, the *John of Dublin*; there were certainly many McDowells aboard both ships, though Ephraim's name does not appear on the *George and Ann*'s passenger list. The voyage took more than four months and ended off course, at Cape Cod instead of Philadelphia; 86 of the ship's 168 passengers died along the way, including 11 McDowells and a child of "widow Mitchell." The McDowells moved first to Lancaster County, Pennsylvania, and then up the Shenandoah Valley in 1737, where they met Benjamin Borden, who hired Ephraim's son John to survey the parcels of land Borden was authorized to patent to settlers farther south in what became Botetourt and then Rockbridge County. Ephraim's younger son James was made a constable of the new Borden Manor. The McDowells were therefore well known in the county, which may account for Ephraim's mention by the court.

We also know a little more about Margaret's husband William. He was the son of John and Mary Mitchell and the brother of John Mitchell Jr. These Mitchells may have known the McDowells in Ireland. Many Mitchells were aboard the *George and Ann* and the *John of Dublin*, and many also settled in Lancaster County, Pennsylvania, before removing to the Valley of Virginia. William and his father or brother John first appear on the muster roll of Captain John Buchanan's company of militia in 1742, with John as the company sergeant and William among the privates. The next year John was made a constable of Borden Manor, taking James McDowell's place, and in the two years after that, William earned the same honor. In 1744, using their father's money, John Jr. bought 400 acres on behalf of their father and mother, John and Mary, on Broad Creek (then called Broad Spring Creek) in what became first Botetourt County and then Rockbridge County.[18] When John and Mary moved to nearby Buffalo Creek in 1746, they sold the 400 acres on Broad Creek to their son William and his wife Margaret. Broad Creek parallels Interstate 81, which

---

[18] Rockbridge County was created in 1791 from southern Augusta and northern Botetourt Counties.

42

crosses the James River a stone's throw from the confluence of Looney's Mill Creek, about 15 miles from the headwaters of Broad Creek. Then in 1752, William and Margaret Mitchell sold their 400 acres on Broad Creek to a Thomas Wilson.

So, in 1752, William and Margaret Mitchell were living along the main north-south road connecting the Ralstons who settled south of the James on Looney's Mill Creek in 1751 and 1753 with the Ralstons living north of the county courthouse in Staunton, to which the Ralstons on Looney's Mill Creek would have had to travel for various legal reasons including claims on land. That a William Mitchell lived along the road to Staunton is attested in the record of a trial of two slaves for murder in 1772: The court ordered that the murderers be hanged and then beheaded and that the head of one be posted "near the road leading from Wm. Mitchell's to Staunton."

William and Margaret Mitchell are worth noting because Margaret's son born in 1753 could have been my fourth-great-grandfather John Sr. if we rethink John Sr.'s year of birth. He is generally assumed to have been born about 1770, but that date assumes he was at least 20 years old when his sons John Jr. and William were born between 1791 and 1794. He could easily have been much older, as many frontier fathers were after the Revolutionary War. Many men born in the 1750's came of age before the war and went off to war before getting married. After the war, many of them also scrambled west to claim land, establish a viable farm, and build at least a cabin for their brides. Then they got married.

A good example is James Mitchell of Robertson County, Tennessee, whom many assume to have been the Robertson County John Sr.'s brother. James was born in 1754, was married in Kentucky sometime after the war, fathered three sons there between 1790 and 1805, and then moved to Tennessee in 1810, where he died in 1835 at the age of 80. John Sr. could have done the same if born in 1753. If he had, he would have been a very reasonable 65 when he died in 1818, instead of just 48 if born in 1770.[19] All things considered, his being born in 1753 makes more sense than his being born in 1770.

---

[19] His year of death is inferred from his last appearance in county records in 1817 and his absence from the 1820 census.

◆

Rethinking John Sr.'s birth year allows us to also rethink his possible paternity among the available Ralstons, one in particular: William Ralston Jr. was born about 1735 and therefore about 18 in 1753. He later married a woman named Rosanna and fathered three children by her named James, Sarah, and Margaret. In 1758, when William was about 23, Rosanna was accused of theft, and the county court declared both her and him "persons of ill fame." William appears to have left Rosanna soon afterwards, for in 1759 Rosanna complained in court that he was not providing for their children, and in 1766 she was using another last name when complaining in court that her children had been taken from her by two men, probably acting as agents of the court. William also remarried but seems to have lived happily ever after, inheriting his father's land and fathering at least four more sons, but none named John, before he died in 1811.

So here we have yet another suspicious coincidence—a Mitchell wife of questionable virtue and a Ralston man of ill fame in his youth, living not far from each other in the Forks of the James, as the area was known, the Mitchell wife along the road certainly traveled by the Ralston man about the time the woman conceived a son whose birth was a court's concern.

Intrigued by the possibilities, I gave in to curiosity and paid FamilyTreeDNA to upgrade my DNA sample to the Big Y–700 level of analysis, charting 700 genetic markers instead of my original 111, in the hope that extra data might at least tell me which of the descendants of early American Ralstons are closest to me genetically. The results, however, as explained to me by Ed Ralston, effectively ruled out my direct descent from any known Ralston, including William Ralston Sr. of Virginia. It appears now that the connection between Mitchells and Ralstons occurred much earlier and not in America. In that case, it is possible that their original union was legitimate, the change of names occurring through remarriage or adoption. It is also possible that the connection between them was indirect, with a generation or two bearing another surname between Mitchell and Ralston, and that both Mitchells and Ralstons descend from a common father by another name. It is even possible that a Mitchell began the Ralston line instead of the other way around.

The last possibility is more likely than one might think. I myself had thought it obvious that 3 Mitchells and 28 Ralstons out of 48 men related by yDNA indicated a common Ralston forefather with a few strays bearing other surnames resulting from "non-paternity events." But there are several reasons why this might not be so.

One reason is the size and self-selective basis of the sample. It may be that Ralstons are over-represented in the sample because of concerted efforts by Ralstons to solve the mystery of who descends from whom among a small group of men bearing a famous but unusual name with so many different spellings. The Ralstons behind the Ralston Project are indeed very active—much more active than the people responsible for FamilyTreeDNA's Mitchell Project. Besides active efforts by project members to recruit men to be tested, there is also the likelihood that just having a rare yet famous surname with so many different spellings makes one wonder more about one's lineage. Genealogical research would also be easier and more rewarding than it would be for someone named Mitchell. Common surnames are much less likely to indicate common ancestors, especially surnames originating as common occupations like Smith or as popular Christian names like Mitchell (from Michael). Ralstons, on the other hand, are more likely to succeed in establishing relations to other Ralstons, which gives them greater incentive to test their DNA.

Second, the number of men of a particular lineage with a particular surname can vary greatly over time. Some generations are more prolific than others, and some fathers father many more sons than daughters. Of the seven certain generations of my own line, just two produced more than three males (Jack's and Ben's). In the century before Jack's birth, William Ralston Sr. appears to have fathered six or seven sons, ensuring the survival of his name for generations to come. If, therefore, a hundred years before him, William Sr.'s great-great-grandfather was fathered by a Mitchell but raised as a Ralston and then went on to father as many Ralstons as William Sr., the original Mitchell's Ralston descendants could easily outnumber his Mitchell descendants to this day.

Third, the more prolific a line is, the more genetic mutations it is likely to generate. This would account for the genetic distance between the Ralstons and the Mitchells, Youngs, Abstens, and Baxters. The

45

Ralstons have all seen more mutations than the others and are themselves divided by mutations into four *subclades* (or subgroups), whereas the common Ralston *haplogroup* (I-BY194140) is a subclade of the earlier or "upstream" Mitchell-Absten-Baxter haplogroup (I-BY120159), which in turn is a subclade of the upstream haplogroup to which the Youngs belong (I-BY61820). The common Ralston haplogroup (I-BY194140) is estimated to have come into being around 1670; the Mitchell-Absten-Baxter haplogroup (I-BY120159) is estimated to have come into being around 1400, plus or minus 180 years and therefore possibly before the adoption of surnames, as the variety of surnames within the group suggests. (For this reason, Ed Ralston believes the I-BY120159 haplogroup is more likely to have come into being before rather than after 1400.) Consequently, the absence of any Ralstons in the upstream group and of any Mitchells, Abstens, Baxters, or Youngs in the downstream group suggests that the former descend from the latter—Ralstons from Mitchells, Abstens, Baxters, or Youngs—rather than the other way around, although the rather limited sample of fully tested men prohibits us from drawing that conclusion.

Fourth, in status-conscious Britain, people long ago often changed their surnames to associate themselves with persons of higher rank. Thus did William Hychyns (Hitchins) become William Tyndale. Thus also did Oliver Williams become Oliver Cromwell. Similarly, with *Mitchell* being (like *Williams*) a common patronym borne by no one especially noteworthy before the nineteenth century, an ambitious seventeenth-century Mitchell might have assumed the grander Ralston surname of his wife, mother, uncle, cousin, or benefactor.

For these reasons, a Ralston originator of Mitchells seems rather unlikely, and a Mitchell originator of Ralstons cannot be ruled out.

◆

What about the Ralstons?

The name *Ralston* is one of many similarly spelled names from the British Isles. Their common ending is from the Old English word *tun* meaning an enclosed plot of land such as a farm, settlement, manor, villa, village, or, of course, town (towns often beginning as settlements that have grown up around farms). The first syllable is the owner's name, either *Ralph*, *Rolf*, or the Norwegian *Hróald*. (The last is very rare in England and possibly confused with the Norman French pronunciation of *Harold* accenting the second syllable.) There are seven English placenames resembling *Ralston*, including Rolstone, Rollestone, Roulston, Rowlston, and Rowlstone. There was also once a Scottish barony of Ralston, seated near Paisley, southwest Glasgow, in Renfrewshire (originally Lanarkshire), and there is today a Ralston neighborhood and a Ralston Golf Club just a mile or so east of the center of Paisley, off the Glasgow-Paisley Road (A761).

Long ago, there was presumably a Ralph of such rank that he obtained a lease on land outside Paisley, making the land "Ralph's tun," whose inheritors were thus known as *de Ralstoun* as early as the thirteenth century.[20] The first on record was *Jacobus de Rauliston* (James Ralston) in 1219. Family tradition holds that the original Ralph was a scion of the MacDuffs who were for a long time the Earls of Fife, but he might rather have been the Ralph who was the chaplain of Paisley Priory and owned land in the area in the late twelfth century. Either way, the early Ralstons were closely tied to the Stewarts, whose progenitor was Walter FitzAlan, an English lord of Breton descent who came to Scotland in 1142 with King David I of Scotland.[21] This Walter served King David as the first High Steward of Scotland and was rewarded with lordship over much of southwest Scotland, including Renfrewshire and Paisley. As the local lord, Walter chartered the founding of Paisley Priory on his land in 1162.[22]

Several thirteenth-century men of rank bore the name *de Rauliston* (by some such spelling). One was Count of Lanark (near Glasgow) when he swore allegiance to Edward I of England in 1296. Many later Ralstons were honored as "Ralston of that Ilk," meaning they were not

---

[20] The word *farm* (from the Latin *firmus*, "firm, solid") refers to a firm lease on land.

[21] *Fitz* comes from the French *fils* meaning "son" and indicates a son without title to property, often illegitimate, although not in Walter's case. The names *Alan* and *Brian* were introduced to England in 1066 by the Breton contingent of William the Conqueror's invasion force. My parents' choice of *Alan* and *Brian* for their two sons was strictly coincidental. They just liked both names.

[22] A priory is a monastery whose abbot resides elsewhere. Paisley Priory became Paisley Abbey in 1245.

just men from Ralston but Ralstons of the Ralston family, descendants of the original Ralph. In time, the Ralstons came to be recognized as a clan by Scotland's Court of the Lord Lyon. There are today four tartans associated with the clan, as well as a crest and a motto: *Fide et Marte* ("With Fidelity and Bravery"). The clan is now classed as armigerous, meaning it has no clan chief, its last having died in 1819.

Several men participating in the Ralston Project are known to be Ralstons "of that Ilk," but most are not of that Ilk and presumably owe their Ralston name to the place and not the family, except perhaps by nonbiological association with the family.[23] Nevertheless, there are many notable Ralstons not "of that Ilk" listed on the Ralston Project's public website (ralstonproject.com), including several descended from three sons of William Ralston Sr. of Botetourt County: John, Samuel, and Matthew.

The most famous Ralston—Ralston Purina—is not in any way connected with any other Ralston of any spelling. That Ralston is an acronym summarizing the self-help pseudo-science of a social reformer named Webster Edgerly (1852–1926), who endorsed the Purina Mills feed-and-cereal company's products. The principles of Edgerly's "Ralstonism" were:

Regime-**A**ctivity-**L**ight-**S**trength-**T**emperation-**O**xygen-**N**ature

Yes, Temperation. It's an engineering term used mainly to describe temperature management mechanisms connecting heating and cooling systems. What Edgerly meant by it is anybody's guess.

◆

It happens that the Ralstons participating in FamilyTreeDNA's Ralston Project fall fairly evenly into two unrelated haplogroups designated R-M269 and I-M223. R-M269 includes all Ralstons of that Ilk, half of the Mitchells participating in FamilyTreeDNA's Mitchell Project, and most men in the British Isles: 80 percent in Ireland; 70 percent in Scotland, Wales, and southern England; and 60 precent in the

---

[23] It has been estimated that half of the people bearing clan names in Scotland and Ireland are not descendants of the clan's founding family but of people who were later associated with the clan.

rest of England.[24] These men are believed to descend from all known invaders of the Isles—Normans, Danes, Vikings, Angles, Saxons, Jutes, Romans, Frisians, Celts, Beakers, and even the Neolithic men with roots in the Caucasus who migrated first north and then west after the Ice Age, eventually occupying and dominating all of Europe.

I-M223 (also labelled I2a1b1 and formerly I2a2a) includes the Ralstons not of that Ilk, me and my two Mitchell matches, one in twenty Mitchells in the Mitchell Project, and the small minority of men in Europe and the British Isles whose male line stretches back to the Mesolithic, Cro-Magnon men known as the Western Hunter-Gatherers, who inhabited southern Europe during the Ice Age. These were the first permanent inhabitants of Northern Europe—light-eyed, dark-haired, medium-skinned men who moved gradually north with the melting glaciers into uninhabited land roughly 14,000 years ago. Among them was the 9,000-year-old Cheddar Man, Britain's oldest complete human skeleton, found in Gough's Cave in Cheddar Gorge, Somerset, in 1903. Of men today, I-M223 includes just 11 percent in southern Scotland, 10 percent in Ulster, 8 percent in East Anglia, 7.5 percent in Cheshire and Lancashire on England's northwest coast, 6.5 percent of men in the Scottish Highlands, 5 to 2 percent in the rest of England and Ireland, and roughly 4 percent in Germany, Denmark, Belgium, and the Netherlands.

There is a matching Mesolithic maternal haplogroup of mitochondrial DNA (mDNA or mtDNA) designated U5 that includes 8.5 percent of the population of Britain and Ireland, where I-M223 men are just 4.5 and 5 percent, respectively. U5 is found in greater and more even percentages throughout Europe, so some of the difference between the survival of male and female Cro-Magnon genes in the British Isles can be explained by successive invasions of people already bearing R-M269 yDNA but U5 mDNA. But this combination of Neolithic yDNA and Mesolithic mDNA is itself explained by a common occurrence

---

[24] These percentages are based on over 15,000 tested, with over 5,000 tested in England, Scotland, and Ireland each. The information on haplogroups in this section is from the website Eupedia.com, at https://www.eupedia.com/genetics/britain_ireland_dna.shtml#romans and https://www.eupedia.com/europe/Haplogroup_I2_YDNA.shtml.

49

contributing to the lower survival rate of Cro-Magnon yDNA compared to Cro-Magnon mDNA: Conquerors conquer more women among the vanquished and breed more children by them, thereby displacing the yDNA of the vanquished while perpetuating the mDNA of the same.

The combined effect of many centuries of conquests and migrations from the Continent to the British Isles was therefore to lower the prevalence of I-M223 in the Isles and to confine its survival to men of lower status. This helps explain differences in its present prevalence in various parts of the Britain and Ireland. Its present higher prevalence in Ulster, Cheshire, and Lancashire is largely explained by migration from southern Scotland to Ulster in the seventeenth century and to Cheshire and Lancashire during the Industrial Revolution of the late eighteenth and early nineteenth centuries.[25] Its present lower prevalence in the Scottish Highlands is partly explained by ancient settlement of the Highlands and Islands by Scandinavians and by the much later migration of poorer Highlanders south to the Lowlands and elsewhere, particularly during the Highland Clearances of the early Industrial Revolution, which saw many Highlanders evicted from their glens to make room for sheep to supply the woolen mills of England. All of these emigrations of lower-status males from Scotland would have changed the genetic balance in Scotland to favor the haplogroups of higher-status males whose ancestors arrived in Scotland later.

Finally, rare as I-M223 is, there is within it a much, much rarer subclade labelled L623 that is believed to have originated some 4,700 years ago and is found nowhere else in Europe except among men whose ancestors were from southern Scotland or Ulster. I and all of my Big Y–700 matches belong to L623.

---

[25] Until 1974, Cheshire and Lancashire included the major industrial cities of Liverpool and Manchester, which are now independent.

CHAPTER 5

As Far as I Will Go

So far, with the help of DNA, we have extended our knowledge of Bellsburg Mitchell ancestry just one generation, to John Mitchell Sr. of Robertson County, the father of both John Mitchell Jr. of Robertson County and my third-great-grandfather William Mitchell of Robertson and then Dickson Counties. We have also established a genetic link to many Ralstons in America, but it is a link so distant that it returns us to our search for Mitchell forebears with few clues as to where to start. There were so many John Mitchells in colonial America and so many of them moving about before and after the Revolutionary War that tracing any one of them across the Appalachians is exceedingly difficult, even if one were to limit the search to John Mitchells from Virginia and North Carolina.

Doubtful of the likelihood of further progress and anxious to move on to other projects, I gave up the search and forced myself to complete the promised report in November of 2021. I even put the report in print and ordered fifteen copies for family members, hoping to have them distributed before Christmas. They did not arrive in time, and even if they had I would not have given them out, because shortly after ordering them I began to regret leaving several curious stones unturned. What was that 1749 Moores v. Mitchells case of slander all about? Why, in 1753, did the Augusta County court examine William's wife Margaret and note only that she had a son? And how is it that after 1753 the only Margaret Mitchell who appears in Augusta County records was the wife not of William Mitchell but of a John Mitchell?

The little that I knew in each case had come from Lyman Chalkley's 1912 extracts of Augusta County court records. What about the actual records still in the Augusta County courthouse? How could I finalize my conclusions without consulting them?

I couldn't, so I hired Janie Sherman, a professional genealogist in Staunton, Virginia, to check the records to see what they might reveal. Janie failed to find any mention of the 1749 case of slander or the 1753 examination of Margaret Mitchell, but she did find a 1753 court order for David Moore and Israel Christian to pay William Mitchell "or his heirs, executors, administrators, or assigns" the sum of £46 for unspecified "damages," pending the result of a suit brought by Moore the same day in which Moore alleged that William Mitchell owed him 23 pounds and 2 shillings but had "absconded" before he could be served papers demanding payment.

The sums of money involved make it likely that this 1753 dispute between William Mitchell and David Moore, and possibly also the 1749 case of slander brought by the Moores against the Mitchells, was over land, possibly the 200 acres near Moore's Creek that William and Margaret Mitchell had claimed in 1746 (while already owning 400 acres farther south on Broad Creek), which they sold in 1748 to a James McClung. Whatever as at issue, it seems now that William did indeed abscond or otherwise disappear after selling his land on Broad Creek in 1752 and that the court in 1753 examined William's wife Margaret about William's whereabouts and about his heirs in an attempt to settle his estate. That would explain why Margaret and not William was examined and why the court noted that Margaret had a son, because Virginia law at the time recognized the right of agnatic primogeniture, according to which the estate of a man who dies intestate (i.e., without a will) goes not to his wife but to his eldest son.[26]

---

[26] The ancient right of primogeniture provided intergenerational continuity of land ownership and social standing, minimizing societal turbulence by having eldest sons assume both the rights and the responsibilities of their fathers. Partible inheritance tends to increase societal turbulence as well as cultural insecurity by dividing estates among all heirs, thereby preventing any one of them from assuming the same social standing as their father.

It would also explain why we hear no more of William and Margaret Mitchell after 1753. Instead, in 1769, we hear of "John Mitchell and his wife Margaret Mitchell" selling 170 acres on Buffalo Creek, where William's parents, John and Mary, bought 400 acres in 1746. William's brother John seems to have married his brother's widow and inherited their parents' land, where he would remain, appearing on annual tax lists as constable for the Buffalo Creek district through 1775.

No William Mitchell appears on the same tax lists, but in 1772, a John Mitchell, William Mitchell, and John Mitchell Jr., in that order, witnessed the will of a neighbor named Paul Whitley, who also lived along Buffalo Creek in 1767 and who later moved to North Carolina. It is possible that these Johns were Margaret's William's father and brother, but their father's likely age at the time (at least 70) makes it more likely that they are Margaret's William's brother and nephew, or perhaps brother and son. And if William disappeared for good in 1753, the William who witnessed the will in 1772 was not Margaret's husband but either her son or her stepson.

We know that there were younger Mitchells named John and William in Augusta County at the time, because in 1765 a John and a William Mitchell both obtained marriage licenses. The county did not record brides' names at that time, but county land records tell us that a John and Sarah Mitchell sold land to a George Wilson in 1768 and that a William and Rebecca Mitchell sold land to a George Peery in 1773.

A generation later, a similar coincidence occurred, when in 1780 another John and William Mitchell obtained marriage licenses in Botetourt County, formerly part of August County—John to Agnes Whitley, daughter of Jonathan Whitley, and William to Jean Mitchell, daughter of another John Mitchell. These marriages are probably too early for the grooms to be the sons of the John and William married in 1765, but they could have been the sons of John and Margaret or even William and Margaret. The John who married Agnes Whitley is likely the son of John or William, as her father Jonathan Whitley is known to have lived along Buffalo Creek in 1767. The William who married Jean Mitchell could be William the son of Thomas Mitchell of Augusta County, who was the eldest son of another John Mitchell, of Beverley Manor, north of Borden Manor (of whom more will be said in the next chapter). That William is mentioned in Thomas's 1806 will. His bride, Jean, could be the daughter of John and Margaret Mitchell of Buffalo Creek.

At least one William Mitchell in the Upper Valley does appear to have had a father or son named John at that time, for in 1783 the Augusta County court determined that a William Mitchell was "heir-at-law" of a John Mitchell who died in 1781 at the Siege of Ninety Six in South Carolina, very likely because he was the deceased's father.[27] The case involved a man alleged to be John Mitchell who was also alleged to have "died a natural death at David Frame's stillhouse" in Augusta County in 1783. After hearing testimony from witnesses to the siege, the court decided the dead man was not William's John.

One even later mention of Virginia Mitchells named John and William seems certainly to involve the sons or grandsons of John or William, the sons of John and Mary: In 1791, John and Nancy Mitchell of York County, South Carolina, granted a Thomas Mitchell power of attorney to sell 400 acres along Buffalo Creek adjacent to land owned by William Mitchell and also "being the tract on which William Mitchell now lives." The sale was completed the following year for £100, with John Mitchell further identified in the record of the sale as "late of Rockbridge County, Virginia," that part of Botetourt County having become part of Rockbridge County the same year as the sale.[28]

◆

The certain movement of John and Nancy Mitchell from Rockbridge County, Virginia, to York County, South Carolina, brings other Mitchells into view, in particular the John Mitchell who appears in the federal census for Mecklenburg County, North Carolina, with a young wife in 1790, then with a young wife and two boys under ten in 1800, and then does not appear in later census records for the county. This Mecklenburg County John could very well be John Mitchell Sr. of Robertson County, Tennessee. Jack Mitchell did tell census takers that his father William and his mother Mary were both born in North Carolina. Mary certainly was born there (she said so twice).

---

[27] Ninety Six is a place, not a date.
[28] The pound remained the currency of the Commonwealth of Virginia until 1793.

Researchers have always assumed that John Sr. was young based on the ages of his sons; the Mecklenburg County John was certainly young: The 1800 census shows him and his wife as being between the ages of 16 and 26 in 1800, which means they were no more than 16 in 1790 and therefore born about 1774.[29] They were still in Mecklenburg County in 1800 but not there in 1810 and could have moved before then to Robertson County, Tennessee, where records show John Sr. buying land as early as 1808. The Mecklenburg County John also had two sons born in the 1790's, which fits with John Sr.'s two sons being born in the early 1790's and coming of age before 1812, when three Mitchells—John Sr., John Jr., and William—signed the petition opposing the building of a jail in Springfield.[30]

The Mecklenburg County John might also have been the son of the aforesaid John and Nancy Mitchell of York County, South Carolina, who sold the land on which a William Mitchell was living on Buffalo Creek in Rockbridge County, Virginia, in 1791. York County, South Carolina, borders Mecklenburg County, North Carolina, where the city of Charlotte is today. The northern portion of York County had, in fact, been part of Mecklenburg County before the boundary between the Carolinas was fixed in 1772. Even today, a corner of York County extends north to the southern edge of Charlotte, just east of the Catawba River, which flows through Mecklenburg and into York. The aforesaid Paul Whitley of Botetourt County, Virginia, bequeathed his land "on the Cattopa [Catawba] in north Carolina" to his sons in his 1772 will, witnessed by three Botetourt/Rockbridge County Mitchells—John, William, and John Jr., in that order. One or both of these John Mitchells seem certain to have settled later in the same area, along the Catawba but in what became South Carolina instead of North Carolina.

A John Mitchell, presumably Nancy's husband, appears in York County in the 1790 census, heading a household including another

---

[29] Such an age for a married couple was not unusual among Scots and Scotch-Irish. Leyburn writes, "Even after the Reformation the age of marriage was often as early as fourteen for boys and twelve for girls." See James G. Leyburn, *The Scotch-Irish: A Social History* (Chapel Hill, N.C.: The University of North Carolina Press, 1962), p. 30.

[30] Full majority was reached at 21, but males could enlist in the militia at 16 and witness legal documents at 14.

male over 16, a male under 16, four females, and no slaves. This John Mitchell is likely to have been the John Jr. who witnessed Paul Whitley's will in 1772, as the elder John who witnessed the will—the son of John and Mary and the brother of Margaret's William—would have been about 70 years old in 1790, whereas the John Jr. who witnessed the will would have been at least in his mid-thirties in 1790 and therefore old enough to have been the father of the sixteen-year-old Mecklenburg County John.

If the John Jr. who witnessed Paul Whitley's 1772 will was the father of the Mecklenburg County John, and the Mecklenburg County John was John Sr. of Robertson County, Tennessee, then we can reasonably add three more generations to our genealogy: John and Nancy, John and Margaret, and John and Mary.

The connection of all these John Mitchells in Virginia, North Carolina, South Carolina, and Tennessee is far from certain, but at least seven facts point toward it:

(1) My distant but definite genetic connection to the settlers of Virginia's Upper Valley, where Ralstons lived not far from Mitchell brothers named John and William and their sons;

(2) The known movement of at least one of the same Mitchells named John to the vicinity of Charlotte, North Carolina, before 1790;

(3) The presence of a younger John Mitchell in the vicinity of Charlotte, North Carolina, in 1790 and with two young sons in 1800 but not there in 1810;

(4) The presence in Robertson County, Tennessee, in 1808 of John Mitchell Sr. with two sons born in the same decade as the sons of the John living near Charlotte in 1800;

(5) The fact that the Robertson County John Sr.'s son William was said by his son John (Jack) to have been born in North Carolina;

(6) The appearance of so many Johns and Williams in three generations of the same Mitchell family of Virginia and then in the next two generations of the same Mitchell family of Tennessee; and finally,

(7) The fact that the Robertson County John Sr.'s son John Jr. and his wife Joanna named their fourth daughter *Nancy*. Scottish custom (followed by many Scotch-Irish) required them to name their first daughter after the mother's mother, the second daughter after the father's mother, and the third daughter after the mother. John Jr. and Joanna might have followed this custom by naming their first three daughters Harriet, Elizabeth, and Frances Joanna, if Joanna's mother was named Harriet and John Jr.'s mother (John Sr.'s wife) was named Elizabeth (instead of the unattested Tabitha). They might then have named their fourth daughter after John Jr.'s fondly remembered grandmother, Nancy.

◆

These pieces do fit rather nicely. Yet there are still several Mitchells unaccounted for, as there always will be. There were five other Mitchell men heading families in Mecklenburg County in 1790, including one named William who was not there in 1800. There were also other Mitchell men in the area whose first names are unknown because they were not living on their own in 1790 and 1800 or because they were living in one of the many counties whose census records were burned by the British in the War of 1812. Some of them could have been John Sr. of Robertson County, but at present we have no other reason to suspect them, just last names and approximate ages.

Among the many Mitchells I do not think worth further research is the John Mitchell of Virginia's Northern Neck who was orphaned in 1776 and released from guardianship when he came of age in 1788. This John's father was James Mitchell (1746–1776) of Richmond and Lancaster Counties in Virginia, who was the son of another John (1710–1759) of Lancaster County, son of a William of Lancaster County and grandson of another William of Accomack County on Virginia's Eastern Shore who died about 1685. Some online genealogies assume the Northern Neck John was the Mecklenburg County John as well as the Robertson County John Sr., but the names and dates make sense for the latter but not for the former. The Mecklenburg County John was too young to be the Northern Neck John—just 14 in 1788, when the Northern Neck John was released from the guardianship of a Richard Mitchell.

Nothing else links the Northern Neck John to Mecklenburg County or Robertson County, and we already have a more plausible explanation for the Mecklenburg John than the sudden marriage and migration of a teenage orphan from Virginia's Northern Neck to southwest North Carolina between 1788 and 1790. We also have DNA data telling us to look elsewhere: Larry Mitchell of Michigan, who got me to test my DNA, is sure that he descends from the Northern Neck Mitchells, but if he is right about that, then we need not look there because Larry is not among my Mitchell matches.

Neither need we look further into the Mitchells of Granville County, North Carolina, some of whom did migrate to Middle Tennessee after the Revolutionary War. Lacking land records for Robertson County, my father was unable to connect our William to our John Sr., so he looked for other Mitchells with sons born in the 1790's and found the widow of Abraham Mitchell of Granville County, who ended her days in Montgomery County, Tennessee. Now we know that William's father was John Sr., and nothing known of John Sr. suggests a connection to the Granville Mitchells. Neither have any descendants of the Granville Mitchells been matched to me, nor does what we know of the Granville Mitchells match the DNA evidence of my ethnic origin.

Whereas the settlers of Granville County appear to have been of English stock, arriving in America as indentured servants in the late 1600's, most of the settlers of Virginia's Upper Valley were Scotch-Irish, as we can see from the map of early plantations on page 38. There are 32 different surnames on the map:

12 Scottish, mostly Lowland and Borderer: *Armstrong, Breckinridge, Buchanan, Cloyd, Howey, Johnston, McNabb, McRoberts, Ralston, Renfro, Snodgrass,* and *Withrow.*

6 English: *Alderson, Cole, Love, Madison, Sayers,* and *Springer.*

5 Irish: *Looney, McClanahan, McDonald, Milligan,* and *Neely.*

5 Common to England, Scotland, and Ireland: *Mitchell, Moore, Preston, Robinson,* and *Smith.*

4 German: *Firebaugh* (Feuerbach), *Kesler, Noffsinger* (Nafziger), and *Reis.*

1   Welsh: *Craddock.*

Nine of these names—*Buchanan, Johnston, Love, McNabb, McRob-erts* (*McRobert*), *Mitchell, Moore, Robinson,* and *Smith*—are known to have been among the original settlers of Ulster from Scotland before 1633. *Armstrong, Looney, Neely, Ralston,* and *Snodgrass* are also often found among the later settlers of Ulster. Given what is known about the settlement of the Shenandoah Valley, we are safe in assuming that the settlers bearing these 14 names were from Ulster and in their own day would have been called "Irish" by their English and German neighbors, even though their grandfathers and grandmothers were from Scotland, England, or Wales. In fact, Beverley Manor and the adjacent Borden Manor were collectively known among Germans in the Valley as the "Irish Tract." But we are less safe in assuming those bearing other names were also from Ulster. *McDonald* is often a Scotch-Irish name, but Bryan McDonald Sr., who appears at the far left of the map, is known to have come not from Ulster but from Wicklow, Ireland, just south of Dublin, in the province of Leinster.

All things considered, it seems that immigration from Ulster accounts for at least half of the names on the map, including William Ralston and David Mitchell. There were already many Mitchells in Virginia in 1739, when David Mitchell swore his Oath of Importation in Orange County, but there were not already many David Mitchells in Virginia at that time. Sixty-two men named Mitchell were transported to the colony of Virginia as indentured servants between 1636 and 1717, but not one of them was named David.³¹ *David Mitchell* was a common Scottish or Welsh combination that only grew in popularity in America with the five great Scotch-Irish migrations between 1717 and 1775.

There was also another family of Mitchells in Augusta County that is known to have come from Lancaster County, Pennsylvania. This was the family of Thomas and Eleanor Mitchell. Thomas's 1734 will identifies him as being "late of Donnegal," which could mean either the county of Donegal in Ulster, Ireland, or the township of Donegal in

---

31 The five most popular first names among the 62 were *Thomas* (16), *John* (9), *William* (6), *Henry* (5), and *James* (4).

Lancaster County, Pennsylvania, which is now known as East Donegal. Thomas's will also names two Johns, his son and his brother, along with his wife Eleanor and four daughters; a William Mitchell witnessed the will. Sometime after Thomas died in Pennsylvania, the family moved southwest to Beverley Manor in Augusta County, Virginia, where in 1747 Thomas's son John settled very near and actually in-between David Mitchell and David's mother Martha, with Thomas's widow Eleanor on her own land a little west of David. Thomas's son John died in 1771, leaving his wife Elizabeth, four sons (Thomas, Robert, John, and James) and two daughters (Eleanor, Mary, and Elizabeth).

These three Mitchell families—David and Martha's, Thomas and Eleanor's, and John and Mary's—moved in the same circles and knew many of the same people. A certain Thomas Wilson connects all three: Thomas and Eleanor's son John married Elizabeth Wilson, Thomas Wilson's sister; John and Mary's son William sold his land on Broad Creek to Thomas Wilson in 1752; and David's sister Eliza married the brother of John Tate, who married Thomas and Eleanor's daughter Mary and witnessed Mary's brother John's will in 1771, along with Thomas Wilson, who died in 1773. A generation later, in 1797, a Thomas Wilson died in Augusta County, leaving a five-year-old orphan named Henry, whom the court bound over to yet another William Mitchell.

It seems likely the three Mitchell families were related in some way. Mary's husband John, the father of John Jr. and William, could very well have been Thomas Mitchell's brother John, named in his will. That would have made John and Mary's sons John and William first cousins of John Mitchell of Beverley Manor, son of Thomas and Eleanor.

At the very least, Thomas's family provides an example of Mitchells in Virginia's Upper Valley emigrating from Ulster, where Ralstons are known to have settled long ago, mostly in the counties of Donegal, Tyrone, and Fermanagh (fer-MAN-uh). Fermanagh is also where the first Ulster colonists named Mitchell settled sometime before 1633. Records from the mid-1800's show high concentrations of Ralstons still in Donegal and Tyrone, with two thirds preferring the spelling

Rolleston or *Rollestone*.[32] The same records also show Mitchells almost everywhere in Ireland but especially in Ulster.

◆

Many Virginia Mitchells and Ralstons moved west after the Revolutionary War to claim land grants for wartime service. They would not have had to have served in the war, only to have purchased the claim of someone who had. William Ralston Sr.'s son John moved to central Kentucky, where he settled just west of Lexington. He might have moved to Ohio before dying sometime after 1800; his son Henry certainly did move to Ohio. William Ralston's son Matthew moved to Tennessee and settled in Jefferson County, east of Knoxville, where he also died sometime after 1800. Matthew's sons and daughters continued westward, ending their days in Hamilton and Marion Counties in East Tennessee and Putnam, Sumner, and Williamson Counties in Middle Tennessee.

James Mitchell of Robertson County also moved west after the war, eventually settling in the northwest corner of the county along the Tennessee-Kentucky line, on Elk Fork Creek, where the county granted him a permit to build a mill. Born in 1754, he would have been in his late twenties when the great post-war migration began in the 1780's. He could have been the James Mitchell who shows up in land records for Davidson County, Tennessee, in 1793, when Davidson included all of the surrounding counties, although one of his sons, Robert B., claimed to have been born in Kentucky in 1798 and to have moved to Tennessee in 1810, when he was 12. The move might have been to be nearer the mill James was building in Robertson County.

John Mitchell Sr. may also have lived a while in Kentucky before buying land in Robertson County, Tennessee, in 1808. He could have been James's brother, but he could not have been James's son. James named three sons in his 1835 will: Robert B., John C., and Samuel F. These sons also had sons in Robertson County, but no descendants of James and his sons have yet been matched to me by yDNA.

---

[32] For facts on the Ralstons of Ulster, I am indebted to Mort Rolleston IV's unpublished paper entitled "The Known Paternal Genealogy of My Georgia and Ballinamallard Rollestons," October 24, 2021.

My father ruled out James and many other Mitchells as the father of our William based on census records, but he never actually ruled out John Sr. He had neither DNA nor the Internet to help him make sense of the scant evidence available to him, and yet he was right about so much—right about all of the children of William Mitchell, right about all the children of Jack Mitchell by his two wives, right about there being two William D. Speights, and right about my mother being his fourth cousin with the first William D. Speight as their great-great-great-grandfather. Though sometimes wrong in his suspicions, he never committed the common crime of amateur genealogists—claiming fallacious relations on flattering but flimsy evidence.

Fortunately for my father, other branches of the family tree were easier to trace even in his day. Our Puritan ancestors have been thoroughly researched by professional historians and genealogists. Our Quaker ancestors wrote lives of their "Friends" just as other Christians write lives of their saints. Our Moravian ancestors wrote their own funeral memoirs (*Lebenslauf*) as an end-of-life accounting of their faith and works. Our Fry ancestors kept a family Bible listing several generations of births, deaths, and marriages. All my father had to do was go back three or fourth generations from his own to establish firm links to what was already established, much of which is now available online, some of which goes back as far as the sixteenth century.

The following pages provide annotated trees of his ancestors, with more information about many of them from his own research and that of others.

John
Mitchell

Mary

John
Mitchell

Margaret

John
Mitchell

Nancy

John Mitchell Sr.
b. bef 1775
d. abt 1818

Elizabeth?
Tabitha?

William
Mitchell **(36)**
b. 1791–1794
d. bef 1850

Mary
Stewart? Morris?
1792-185_

William D.
Speight
ca. 1780- **(35)**

Albert Speight
1800-

John Tillman
Mitchell **(37)**
1827-1899

Martha A.
Speight
1832-186_

Benjamin
Wesley
Mitchell **(38)**
1863-1916

Sarah Allie
Fry **(18)**
1870-1934

John Tillman
Mitchell, Sr. **(39)**
1903-1964

Alma Altha
Morris **(40)**
1907-1994

John Tillman
Mitchell, Jr. **(41)**
1926-1990

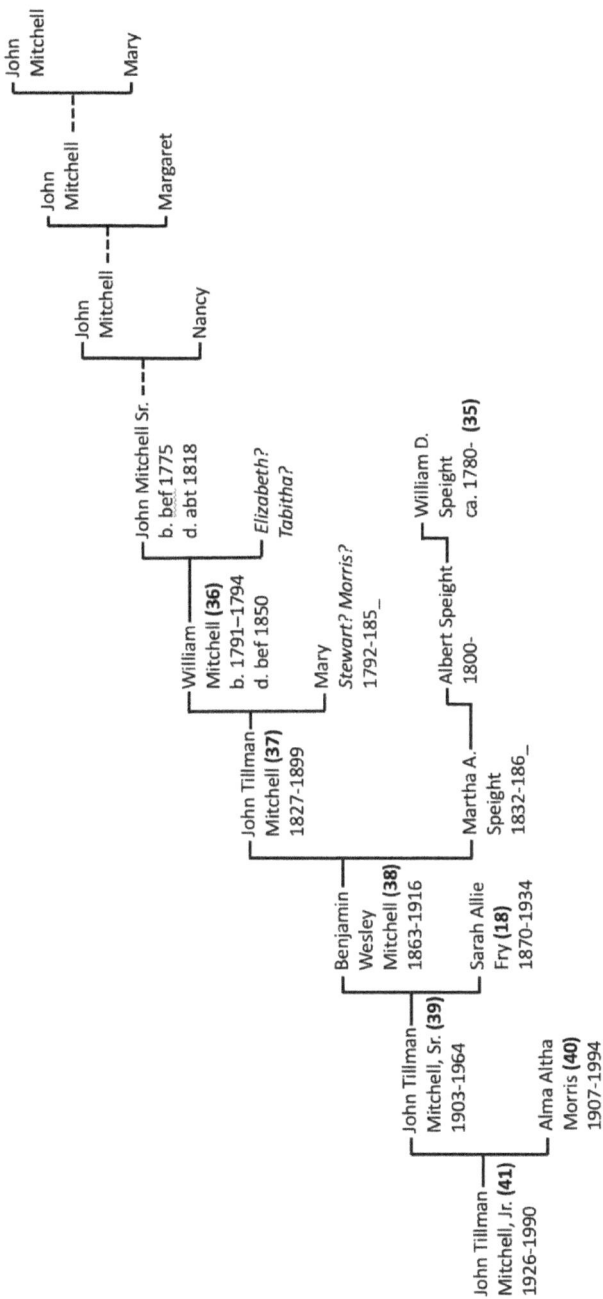

Figure 5: Paternal Ancestors of John Tillman Mitchell, Jr.

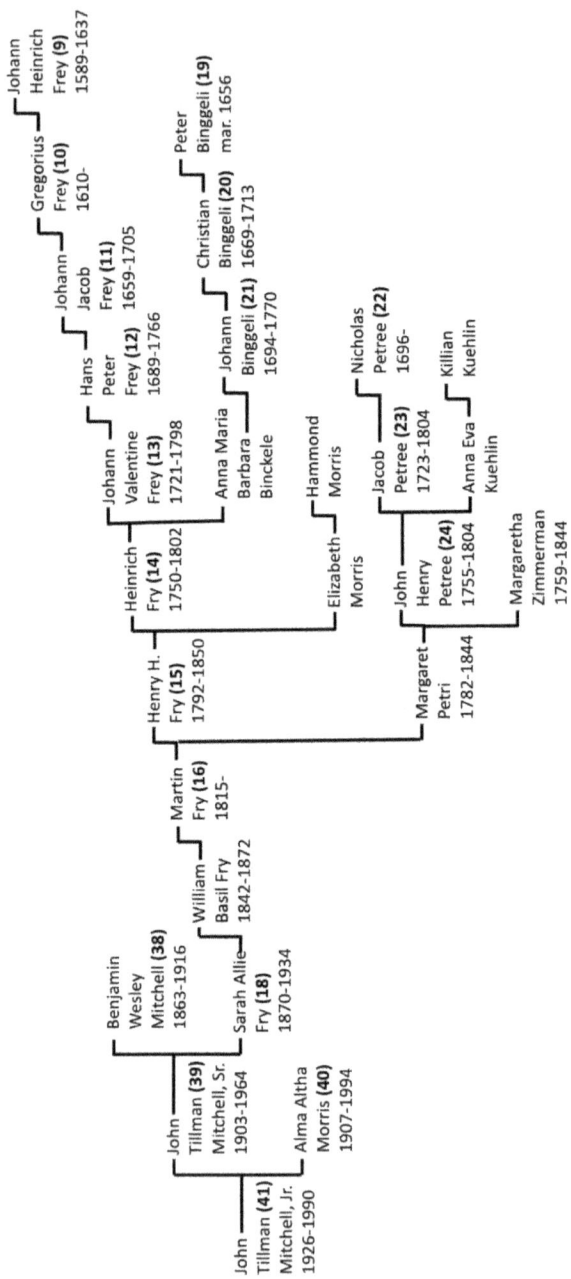

Figure 6: Maternal Ancestors of John Tillman Mitchell, Sr.

64

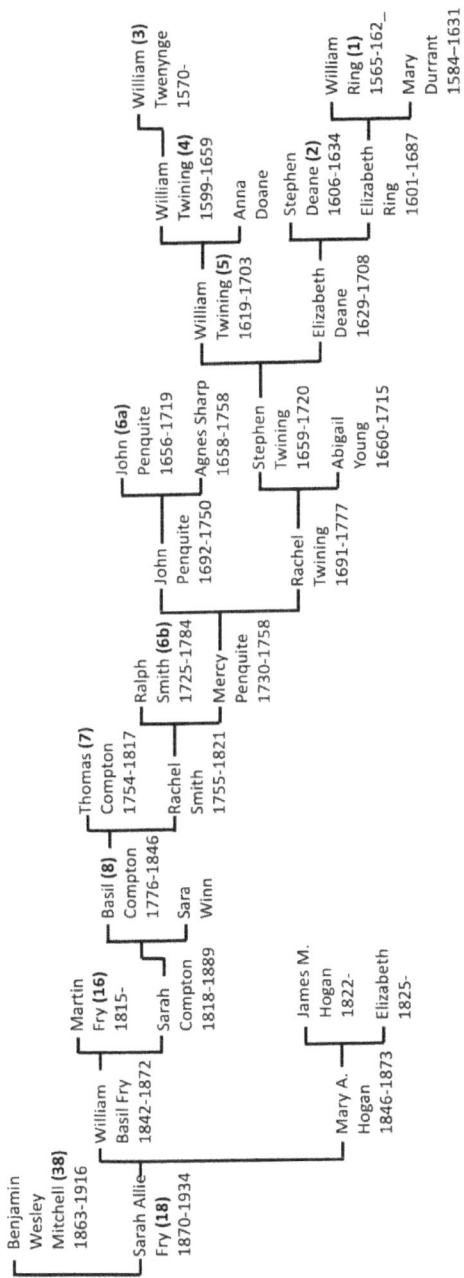

Figure 7: Maternal Ancestors of John Tillman Mitchell, Sr.

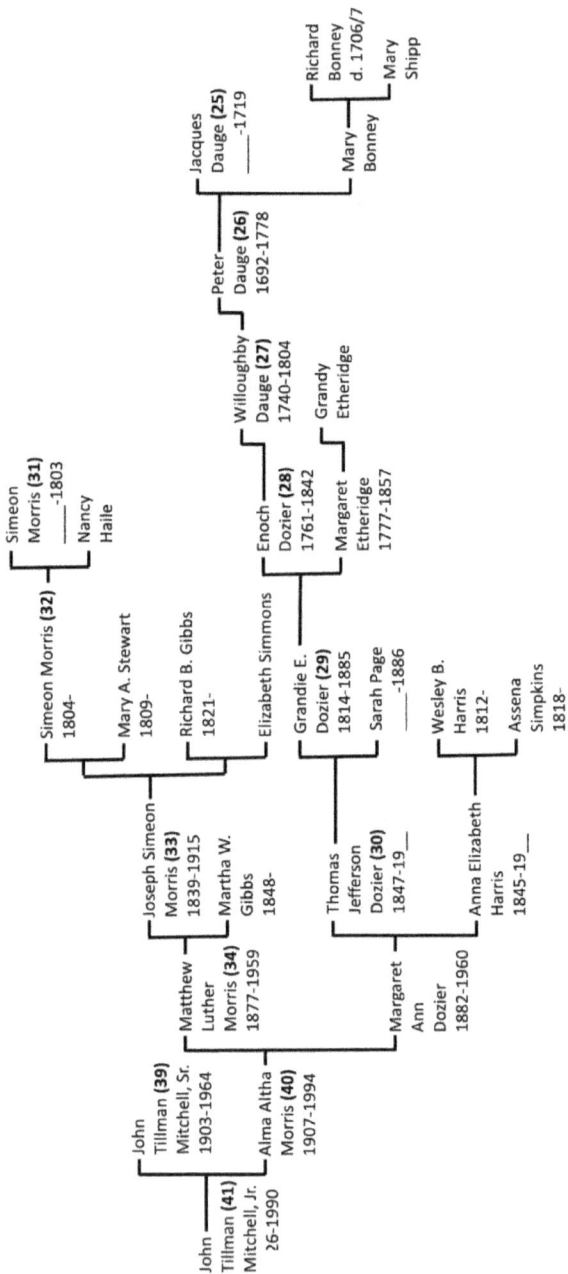

Figure 8: Maternal Ancestors of John Tillman Mitchell, Jr.

66

Leaves on the Family Tree

1. William Ring, a weaver by trade, born in Pettistree, Suffolk, England, in 1565; died between 1620 and 1629 in Leiden, Zuid-Holland, Netherlands. Wife **Mary Durrant**, born in Ufford, Suffolk, England; died 1631 at Plymouth. The Ring family were part of the original Separatist community in Holland that sailed for the New World aboard the *Mayflower* and the *Speedwell* on August 23, 1620. The next day the *Speedwell* sprang a leak, forcing both ships to return to port. Robert Cushman, another passenger aboard the *Speedwell*, wrote in his diary, "Poore William Ring and my selfe doe strive who shall be meate first for the fishes, but we look for a glorious resurecion." The *Mayflower* left again alone on September 6, and the Rings returned to Holland. William died there, but Mary and their daughter **Elizabeth** joined the Separatists in Plymouth Colony around 1629.

2. Stephen Deane (1606–1634), arrived at Plymouth Colony in 1621 aboard the *Fortune*, the first ship to land at Plymouth after the *Mayflower*. He missed the Pilgrims' first Thanksgiving feast by a few weeks. Wife **Elizabeth Ring**, born in Ufford, Suffolk, England, in 1601. Both died at Plymouth Colony, Stephen in 1634 and Elizabeth in 1687. Also on the *Fortune* were Robert Cushman, who was with William Ring aboard the *Speedwell*, and Philipe de la Noye, another Separatist aboard the *Speedwell*, who founded the Delano family of America, from which Franklin Delano Roosevelt descends through his mother, Sara Ann Delano.

3. William Twenynge, born 1570 in Painswick, Gloucestershire, England. The surname is a place name from Twyning, Gloucestershire.

4. William Twining, born 1599 in Gloucester, England; died 1659 in Eastham, Barnstable, Massachusetts. Wife **Anna Doane**, born 1600 in Manchester, Lancashire, England; died 1680 in Eastham, Barnstable, Massachusetts.

5. William Twining, born 1619 in Gloucester, England; died 1703 in Newtown, Bucks Co., Pennsylvania. Wife **Elizabeth Deane**, born 1629, Plymouth, Plymouth Colony, Massachusetts; died 1708 in Newtown, Bucks Co., Pennsylvania. William was a deacon of the First Church of Eastham, which suffered a schism in the late 1600's. William and several others joined the Quakers and moved to Pennsylvania in 1695. (His daughter Meritable married Daniel Doane, another who also joined the Quakers. President Richard Nixon descends from that line.)

6a. John Penquite (1656–1719) immigrated from St. Keyne's parish in Cornwall, England, in 1683, and was the third settler in what is now Wrightstown Township, Bucks Co., Pa. He married **Agnes Sharpe** (1658–1758) in 1686. The pair were prominent Quakers, hosting Quaker meetings in their home for many years before a local meetinghouse was built. *Penquite* is a Cornish placename of obscure origin. The River Fowey flows through Penquite Wood to the English Channel, west of Plymouth. St. Keyne's is a few miles east of the wood.

6b. Ralph Hoard Smith (1725–1784) and **Mercy Penquite** (1730–1758) married in Pennsylvania but moved South Carolina with other Quaker pacifists to escape the French and Indian War. It is through Ralph that my sister Dianne was finally able to satisfy the DAR for membership. Some Smith descendants say Ralph died of smallpox while a prisoner of the British, but his death in 1784 means he survived the war. Records of the Wrightstown, Pa., Quaker church list a "Ralph Smith" as the son of a William and Marcey Smith, which William is believed to have emigrated from Yorkshire to Bucks County, Pa., in 1684. But there were other Smiths in the county about that time, including a Ralph Smith named as one of the original settlers of Falls Township, organized in 1692, who may have been the son or grandson of the Ralph Smith who immigrated to Massachusetts in 1633 and died there in 1685.

7. Thomas Compton (1754–1817) bought 200 acres of land on Dutchman's Creek, near Glenn Springs, S.C., southwest of Spartanburg, in 1784. His 1817 will is on record. The name Compton means "hill town." There are several such in England, though some Comptons claim descendancy from the Anglo-Saxon lord Alwyne, a contemporary of Edward the Confessor. Alwyne's son Turchill was the earl of Warwick at the time of the Conquest but sided with the Normans and so was allowed to keep his lands. Turchill's sons took the surname Compton, which was for many years the surname of the earls of Northampton.

8. Basil Compton (1776–1846) moved to Giles Co., Tenn., in 1819. His 1846 will is on record, witnessed by Martin Fry.

9. Johann Heinrich Frey married **Anna Hon** on July 2, 1609.

10. Gregorius Frey married **Verena Oberborfer** on Feb. 7, 1636/37.

11. Johann Jacob Frey was born and died in Wingen, Alsace. He married **Anna Maria Schaub** in 1688 in Wingen.

12. Hans (or Johann) Peter Frey was a tailor born 1689 in Wingen, Alsace, on the present border between France and Germany, near the town of Lemberg. He married **Anna Barbara Schmidt** (1696–1768) in Wingen in 1715, moved to Pennsylvania in 1733, converted with his wife to the Moravians in 1745, moved to North Carolina in 1765, and in 1766 was the first person buried in the "God's Acre" of the Friedberg Moravian Church south of Winston-Salem, N.C. His wife is buried under the name "A. Barb. Frey" in the Moravian cemetery in Bethania, N.C., northwest of Winston-Salem, on her last visit to the church she and her husband had attended for many years.

13. (Johann) Valentine Frey, born in Wingen, Alsace; married the widow **Anna Maria Barbara Binckele Meyer** in East Cocalico Township, Lancaster County, Pa., in 1742; died in Clemmons, N.C., and in buried in the Hope Moravian Cemetery on Chapman Road. His grave is marked with a DAR plaque identifying him as a "Revolutionary Patriot." According to his *Lebenslauf* (funeral memoir), he was raised a Lutheran but converted to the Moravians along with his father and mother while in Pennsylvania. He was a founding member of the Friedberg Moravian congregation but lived his last days with the Hope congregation, cared for by his daughter. His wife was born in 1722 in Alsace, died in Salem (now Winston-Salem), N.C., in 1791, and is buried there in the Salem Moravian Graveyard. The Freys and Binckeles were among the original Pennsylvania Dutch who left Pennsylvania to escape the French and Indian War. Valentine had three sons known by their middle names: Valentine Jr., Michael, and Heinrich. Their first names were all Johann.

14. Heinrich Fry, born at Muddy Creek, in Berks Co., Pa.; died in Stokes Co., N.C. His first wife Sarah Klein died in 1776. His second wife, from whom we are descended was **Elizabeth Morris** (1761–1840+), daughter of **Hammond Morris**.

15. Henry H. Fry, born in Stokes Co., N.C.; died Giles Co., Tenn. Henry married Margaret Petree, daughter of **John Henry Petree** (1755–1804) and **Margaretha Barbara Magdalena Zimmerman** (1759–1844). Henry's first cousin Francis, son of Michael Fry, fled to Texas to escape the law in Tennessee about the time of the Mexican War (1846–1848). For his service in the war, Francis was granted 3,000 acres in Harris County, Texas. Still today there is in Harris County a Fry Road exit off Interstate 10, west of Houston. Francis's heirs died leaving the land unclaimed for many years. About 1940, the Frys of Tennessee hired a lawyer to establish their claim on the estate, which they thought might include oil rights. My father remembered the excitement this caused among his kin at the time. I received from him the 1940 letter from the lawyer to my grandfather, dashing their hopes (there were closer kin with stronger claims on the estate), but also detailing much of the family history, back as far as Hans Peter Frey.

16. Martin Fry, born in 1815 in Stokes Co., N.C.; died in Giles Co., Tenn. He married Sarah Compton (1818–1889), daughter of Basil Compton and Sara Winn. Martin was Francis Fry's first cousin. Martin Fry's Bible records many dates of relevance to the Fry and Mitchell families, including the births of my grandfather, (John) "Tilman Mitchel" on March 6, 1903, and all of his siblings. I have photocopies of the pages.

17. **William Basil Fry** died before his brothers hauled the Fry and **Hogan** families to Texas in covered wagons in the 1870's, possibly to escape an epidemic of tuberculosis, which had claimed several family members, maybe even William himself in 1872. The Hogans moved back to Fulton Co., Ky., before 1880, with William's son Martin Fry and daughter **Sarah Allie Fry**.

18. **Sarah (Sally) Allie Fry** (1870–1934), my father's grandmother, lived in his house until she died, when he was eight. He wrote later:

> I vividly remember her entertaining me for hours with her memories of a wagon-train trek to Texas [in 1877] and return to Tennessee. It is ironic that my age at the time she told me these stories was very close to her age at the time she experienced them. They made a deep impression on me. Little wonder then that one of the four children ultimately broke under the strain.

He described Allie's accounts of accidents and attacks by wild animals as "blood-curdling." The child who supposedly broke under the strain of the move was Allie's older sister Lizzie, who showed signs of insanity. "One night," he wrote, "the family found her standing at the edge of a pond, about to jump. They assumed she had been sleep-walking. She passed away not too long afterward and there is reason to believe that it might have been suicide."

The trek to Texas was made by the extended family, including seven Fry or Hogan uncles, according to my father's aunt Guysell (GUY-zel), one of Allie's daughters. Why would the entire family pick up and move to Texas in 1877? My father first thought it might have been to claim the land left by the late Francis Fry in Harris County, though it appears they only got as far as Dallas, where three of the uncles stayed. He later wondered whether they might have fled Giles County, Tennessee, to escape an outbreak of consumption (tuberculosis), which had claimed four family members in the previous years. Guysell told my father that Allie was obsessed with cleanliness and hawkish about keeping her children away from anyone who was sick, especially Ben West's half-brother Clyde, who died of consumption at age 22. While staying the night at Ben and Allie's, Clyde would be seized by coughing fits and lean out the window to spit out the phlegm; the next morning, Allie would take a shovel, scoop up the soil beneath the window, carry it to the woods, and bury it.

19. Peter Binggeli married **Magdalena Spring** in 1656. Binggeli is a Swiss name, common in Canton Bern.

20. Christian Binggeli (also Binckele, Binkele, and the American Binkley) married **Elisabeth Burri**, daughter of **Jaggi (Jacob) Burri and Elsbeth Zbindon**, in 1693 in Guggisberg, Canton Bern, Switzerland. Guggisberg is famous for its Baby Swiss cheese. One Website for Guggisberg is today maintained by a Stephan Binggeli.

21. Johann Binggeli was born in Guggisberg, Canton Bern, Switzerland, in 1694. He married **Margaretha Weissenbach** in Alsace in 1715 and died in Lancaster, Pennsylvania in 1770 at the age of 76.

22. Nicholas Petree was born in Gemüngen, Rhineland, Germany, in 1696. He married his first wife, Anna Schunchen, in 1719, and his second wife, **Anna Margaretha Schall** from Biebern, Germany, in 1722.

23. Jacob Petree was born to Nicholas and his second wife Anna Margaretha in 1723 in Schönborn, Rhineland, Germany. He immigrated aboard the *Loyal Judith* in 1743 and married **Anna Eva Kuehlin**, daughter of **Killian Kuehlin**, in 1747 in Berks County, Pa. In 1779, he received a grant of 100 acres in Stokes County, N.C., where he lived until his death in 1804. He and his wife are buried at Nazareth Lutheran Church in Rural Hall, N.C., of which he was a founding member. Rural Hall is north of Winston-Salem in Forsyth Co. There is today a Petree Road just west of Winston-Salem.

24. John Henry Petree (1755–1804) married **Margaretha Barbara Magdalena Zimmerman** (1759–1844). His sister Maria Catherine Petree married Johann Valentine Frey Jr. (1748–1814), brother of Heinrich Frey. His daughter **Margaret** married Heinrich's son **Henry H. Frey**, her first cousin.

25. Jacques (James) Dauge (1660–1719) is believed to have been born in France. He first appears in Virginia records in Lower Norfolk County in 1687, suing his neighbor for failure to assist in the building of a road across a swamp. In 1689, he owned 1,034 acres in Lower Lynnhaven Parish, Lower Norfolk Co. In the early 1690s, he married **Mary Bonney**, daughter of his neighbor **Richard Bonney** (d. 1706/7) and **Mary Shipp Bonney**. James appears in Currituck County, N.C., about 1713. James served as sheriff of the county in 1714 and as a captain in the local militia during the Tuscarora War of 1713–14. His will was probated in Princess Anne County, Va., in 1719, and identifies sons John, Richard, William, James & **Peter** and his daughters Mary, Macena, Nowdina & Jacqueline. Witnesses: William & Edward Bonney. Executors his wife and John Bonney. It also lists a 1,025 acre tract of land located on Powell's Point, a spit of land between Albermarle Sound and Currituck Sound, across from Kitty Hawk.

The name *Dauge* is assumed to come from France, possibly from the *pays d'Auge*, the valley of the Auge River in eastern Normandy, south of La Havre. But there are also hamlets and parishes named *Auge* and people surnamed *Dauge* scattered throughout France, from the Ardennes in the northeast to Languedoc in the southwest. The prevalence of the place name may be the work of the Romans, who frequently applied the appellation *Augusta* to towns and colonies. Cologne, Germany, was originally Colonia Augusta, and Zaragoza in Spain was originally Caesar Augusta.

There are also French Doziers, and American Doziers descended from them, through a certain Leonard Dozier of an ennobled family in Berry. But *Dozier* and *d'Auge* are quite different names in French. The second syllable of *d'Auge* is unaccented and barely even pronounced: DOE-zhuh in French and later DOE-zhur in English, whereas the French *Dozier* would be Doe-zee-AY.

Dozier family historians speculate that James Dauge was a French Huguenot, a Calvinist Protestant, who fled France after the 1685 revocation of the Edict of Nantes, which withdrew the edict's grant of religious freedom. The timing would be right for James's appearance in America. The problem is that the only things French about James were his last name and perhaps the name of his daughter Jacquelina. His own first name, his wives' names, the names of his other daughters (Mary, Macina, and Nowdina), and the names of his sons (Richard, Benjamin, John, Peter, William, and James) do not suggest recent French Huguenot ancestry. Maybe James's parents were themselves already English, even if earlier generations of Dauges had been French. (It is certain that the names *Dauge* and *Dozier* are not English.)

My father had somewhere heard that the Dozier family's progenitor was a Frenchman named Enoch Dauge who married an Englishwoman named Anna Bell. I can find no support for this beyond two curious facts: (1) James Dauge was granted 250 acres of his land for paying the passage of three persons: himself, Margaret Dauge, and James Bell. (2) There is a Bell Point on Bell Island in Currituck Sound, off Powell's Point, near Tull's Creek. The name *Enoch* appears among the descendants of James Dauge, but three generations later (see 28 below).

26. Peter Dauge (1692–1778) was born about 1692 in Princess Anne County, Va. Peter moved with his father and brother Richard to Currituck Co., N.C., about 1712–13. Soon thereafter, he married Susannah Tully, daughter of pioneer settler Benjamin Tully. (There is today a Dozier Road between Tull's Creek and Currituck Sound.) Susannah died first, however, and Peter married a second time to **Angelica Gregory** about 1737. Peter's will is online naming all his sons and daughters.

27. Willoughby Dauge (1740–1804) was born in Currituck Co., N.C., about 1740, the son of Peter and Angelico Dauge. He married **Millicent Munden** about 1760 and served as a corporal in the Continental Army during the American Revolution (DAR Patriot Index, 1976). He died in Currituck Co., N.C., in 1804. Millicent might be the daughter of Stephen Munden listed on the county tax roll in 1769. The Mundens were a large family of Quakers living mainly in Perquimans and Pasquotank Counties. A branch of the family moved to Currituck in the 1700s. Munden Point on the North Landing River in Virginia is named for them. The river flows into Currituck Sound.

Willoughby's older brother Peter was a major in the Second Regiment of the Pasquotank Militia in 1776 and eventually rose to the rank of general in the N.C. militia. Peter died at Mt. Pleasant plantation in Camden Co., N.C., in 1801.

28. Enoch Dozier (1761-1842) was born in Currituck Co., N.C., where he married **Margaret Etheridge** (1777–1857), daughter of **Grandy Etheridge**, in 1777. He is known to have moved to Davidson Co., Tenn., and to have exercised the power of attorney in a land sale by relatives from Currituck Co. in a Tennessee court. Enoch and Margaret are both buried in the Haile-Adkisson Cemetery off River Road at Cub Creek, "in a field on the river side of the road," Davidson Co., Tenn. I have photos of their tombstones. Enoch appears on an 1812 militia list for Davidson County as "Enoch Douge" (in Capt. Haile's company, along with Peter Douge), demonstrating a step in the evolution of the spelling of *D'Auge* to *Dauge* to *Douge* to *Dozier* as well as the continuity of the long-O pronunciation the first syllable at all times.

29. Grandy E. (1814–1885) and **Sarah** (Sallie, d. 1886) **Dozier** are buried behind their house on Sam's Creek in Cheatham County. Tom Jeff and Anna Elizabeth (or Grandpap and Grandma Dozier) lived there also, until they moved in with Luther and Maggie Morris. My father remembered visiting the house in the 1930's, when it was owned by Dave Dozier. It was recently (and may still be) owned by Jim Garrett, author of a book on Cheatham County cemeteries.

30. Thomas Jefferson "Tom Jeff" Dozier (1847–19_) was 15 when he was strung up by Yankee foragers, who threatened to hang him—three times, it is said—if he didn't tell them where the horses and hams were hidden. He didn't tell, and they didn't hang him. My grandmother remembered him as a devout member of the Church of Christ.

When a Pentecostal neighbor argued that the Apostles themselves spoke in tongues, Tom Jeff replied, "Yes, and you don't see any of them walking around now, do you?"

31. Simeon Morris married **Nancy Haile** in 1800 and died in 1803, leaving her with two children. This may have been the Morris who once owned Nashville's Capitol Hill and traded it for a mule, although a William Morris who signed the Cumberland Compact in 1780 is also a possibility. *Morris* was a common nickname meaning swarthy or "Moorish." *Haile* is a Scottish spelling of the English *Hale*, which the Hailes of Cheatham County later adopted. The Hailes were among earliest settlers of the county.

32. Simeon Morris Jr. (b. 1804) married **Mary A. Stewart** (b. 1809). The final T in *Stewart* is Scottish, but the English *Steward* is much more common in early census records of Cheatham County.

33. Joseph Simeon Morris (1839–1915) was a private in the Ashland City Guards, Co. E, 18th Tennessee Infantry, from May 1861 to May 1865. Wounded in the head and left for dead at Fort Donelson on Feb. 16, 1862, he came to during the night and walked home, his regiment having surrendered. Six months later, the 18th was paroled in a prisoner exchange, and Joe rejoined it in time to fight in the Battle of Stone's River (Second Murfreesboro), from Dec. 31, 1862, to Jan. 2, 1863. He stayed with the 18th until he was captured at Marietta, Ga., July 3, 1864, just after the very bloody Battle of Kennesaw Mountain, where the 18th anchored the far left of the Confederate line.

I had long suspected that, with the war moving farther and farther from home, Joe deserted and was captured trying to make his way around the Union army. My reason for suspecting this was that he was reported absent without leave (AWOL) by his own unit a few days after the battle and not recorded as captured by the Union army until two or three days later. I have since learned that five days after the battle, Union forces outflanked the Confederates' far left, which forced the whole Confederate army to withdraw to Atlanta. It is therefore possible that Joe was captured by the flanking force while foraging and that his official capture date was when he was formerly processed as a prisoner of war in Marietta two or three days after his actual capture and the Confederate withdrawal.

Joe finished the war as a POW at Camp Douglas, Ill. His oath of allegiance notes that he had blue eyes and stood five feet and five inches. He signed by mark. In 1911, he applied for and received a state pension of $14 a month. His application mentions Fort Donelson, Murfreesboro, Chickamauga, "and the fight from Dalton Ga. to Marietta Ga. New Hope Church, Powder Springs, too." Wesley Speight and B.F. Hannah attested to his service. (Wesley was the younger brother of Jack Mitchell's first wife Martha Speight.) Joe valued his own estate at $250 and his wife's estate at $500. Asked how he supported himself, he answered, "Farming. My boys help me." The examining physician, a Dr. Lenox in Ashland City, reported that Joe suffered from chronic rheumatism and was very deaf.

Jadie Morris, my grandmother's younger brother, told my father of the scar on Grandpa Morris's scalp from his head wound at Fort Donelson, which left a permanent crease from front to back "squarely in the middle of his skull." Jadie also insisted to my father that Joe had served in the Union Army. It is true that the Morrises were anti-slavery, and Joe's younger brother Guilford did indeed serve in a Tennessee regiment of the Union Army, but Jadie was wrong about Joe's military service.

34. Matthew Luther Morris (1877–1959) went by "Lute," though we knew him as "Pappy." The marriage of Lute and **Maggie** or "Mammy" (1882–1960) healed a fabled rift between the Morrises and the Doziers. (The Doziers had owned quite a few slaves, and the Morrises were anti-slavery.) He and Maggie lived in a house on Bradley-Dozier Road, right behind Brantley's Restaurant (now O'Brien's Southern Diner) off Highway 49 in Cheatham County. In their old age, they moved in with Granddaddy and Grandmother on Lischey Avenue in East Nashville. In an interview with a Nashville newspaper, Mammy and Pappy told the story of the family once owning Tennessee's Capitol Hill. They also said they never had to pay money for meat, dairy, or vegetables until the 1940's. They raised nearly everything they ate on their farm. (The house behind Brantley's was taken over by Uncle Jess

Reed and Bob Reed. My father saw it decay into nothing over time, "some of it [went] up the chimney.")

35. William D. Speight was my father's great-great-great-grandfather through his son **Albert** (b. 1800) and my mother's great-great-great-grandfather through his son **William D.** (1811–1852), making my father and my mother fourth cousins. *Speight* is a Yorkshire word for woodpecker. The German word for woodpecker is *specht*, which is also sometimes a surname.

36. William Mitchell appears in the records of Robertson County, Tennessee, in 1812, having been born between 1791 and 1794 (in North Carolina, according to his son Jack). As the second son, he received much less of his father's estate than his brother John Jr. The 1820 census shows John Jr. owning four slaves and William owning just one, whom he might have sold to buy the farm near Cheap Hill in 1824 or to buy his farm across the Cumberland near Bellsburg before 1830, as the 1830 and 1840 censuses show him owning no slaves.

37. The first **John Tillman Mitchell** (1827–1899) in the family was variously known as John, J.T., and finally Jack. He is buried in the Mount Liberty churchyard in Dickson Co. In colonial America, *Tillman* was also spelled *Tilmon* and *Tilghman*. It is an English surname meaning either a tiller of soil or a maker of tiles. *Tilmon* was a popular first name in the late 1700's and early 1800's. Much has already been said of his politics and temperament. Little else is known about him, and no photos of him are known to exist.

38. Benjamin Wesley Mitchell (or Ben West, as he was known) (1863–1916) died of typhoid fever in July 1916. Six months later, his house burned down, and his widow and younger children, including 13-year-old Tillman, went to live with an older brother. Ben West is buried in the Mount Liberty churchyard in Dickson Co. His brother Dave (Jefferson Davis, also known as Jiff) and his half-brothers Clyde and Walter are buried there, too.

39. John Tillman Mitchell, Sr. (1903–1964) My grandfather's headstone at Nashville's Spring Hill Cemetery says "J. Tillman," and his parents and siblings always called him "Tillman." His three sons called him "Daddy," and his grandchildren called him "Granddaddy," but his wife, Alma, always called him "Pete." It was a pet name she had picked for him when they courting. She told me she was waiting for him one evening on the steps of the Greenbrier Church of Christ in Cheatham County, and when she saw him coming, she called out, "Hey there, Pete," for no particular reason. Afterwards told him, she told him, "I'm gonna call you 'Pete' from now on," and she did. He called her "Miss Alma" all her life. He was an expert crane operator on the Cumberland River in Nashville. Often called upon to handle the hardest jobs, he earned enough to build a four-bedroom bungalow at 1408 Lischey Avenue in East Nashville in 1936, in the midst of the Great Depression. He liked to hunt and to sing. His favorite hymn was "Seeking the Lost," no doubt because the basses take the lead in the chorus:

> *Going afar upon the mountains,*
> *Bringing the wanderer back again*
> *Into the fold of my Redeemer,*
> *Jesus the Lamb for sinners slain.*

They say he sometimes played a squeeze-box (accordion or concertina) and sometimes also the inexpensive six-string Stella guitar that my father inherited, which I have had restored to playable condition. He liked his coffee served in a saucer instead of a cup. "Saucer that coffee, Miss Alma," he'd said. I barely knew him but remember him as a big, quiet, kindly man who teased us gently and gave us Juicy Fruit gum. He died of a heart attack after church one Sunday in 1964, at the age of 61.

40. Alma (Altha) Morris Mitchell (1907–1994) Like her maternal grandfather, Tom Jeff Dozier, Grandmother Alma was a lifelong member of the Church of Christ with strong views about religion, all very reasonable and traditional. She had read the Bible from cover to cover nine times before she died. She deliberately spoiled her husband with fond and respectful service while he was alive and thereby earned from him a free hand in governing the household. She had a talent for management and worked for many years as the lunchroom supervisor for local schools and a church summer camp. Even in her eighties she was running the meal service at the Ashland City seniors center. She fished a lot in retirement and once thought she had caught a record-setting bluegill, but a turtle ate it off the catch line while she continued fishing. (My brother Alan knows the spot.) My father's cousin, Don Mitchell, tells the story of Grandmother setting out boiled custard and whiskey for her Morris and Dozier kin when they visited during the holidays, but setting out only boiled custard when the Mitchells came to visit. When asked, she said that if she set out whiskey for the Mitchells, they would drink only that and there would be none left. She never considered remarrying when Pete died; her church, her children, and her grandchildren were enough for her. She did not struggle to stay alive as long as possible as many people do and instead faced death with great dignity, trusting in the resurrection.

41. John Tillman Mitchell, Jr. (1926–1990) My father was "J.T." to family and friends but "John" at the office. He grew up in East Nashville during the Great Depression, though I never heard him speak of it. His father was always employed, and the family was never in want. He went to East Nashville public schools but spent all his summers in the country with his grandparents. This was fine when he was young, but he resented it as a teenager. At home in town, he learned to play the piano on an old player piano that had had its playing mechanism removed.

After finishing high school in 1944, he was drafted into the Army Air Corps and trained as a B–24 gunner, but he didn't make it overseas until after V-E Day (May 8, 1945), after which he was sent to Germany with an aviation engineering unit. He spent most of his time in Germany supervising a construction crew of German POWs whose main task was pouring concrete to build Rhein-Main Air Force Base, which is now part of the Frankfurt airport. After the war, he attended Vanderbilt University on the G.I. Bill, earning a degree in civil engineering. He married my mother right after graduating and went immediately to work for the U.S. Army Corps of Engineers, starting in the Nashville office and then moving up to the Cincinnati office in 1961. He retired from the Corps as Chief of the Reservoir Control Center of the Ohio Valley Division in 1981 at the age of 55.

Music was always a big part of my father's life. While at Vanderbilt, his high-school classmate Harold Bradley taught him to play the bass fiddle for his swing band. Harold was the younger brother of legendary record producer Owen Bradley. Together the Bradleys founded Quonset Hut Studio (later Columbia Studio B), the first music studio in Nashville's Music Row. Later, they also founded RCA Studio A, with country-music star Chet Atkins. Owen now has a park named for him in Music Row. Harold was a popular studio musician, playing for Patsy Cline, Roy Orbison, Elvis Presley, Willie Nelson, Bob Dylan, Joan Baez, Slim Whitman, and the Byrds.

My father belonged to the musicians' union and played for Harold through college and a while afterwards before giving it up to be home more after his children were born. He continued playing the piano and later the organ at home, and he sang for a while in a barbershop quartet. He made sure to give all of his children an opportunity to learn music.

He was a member of the Church of Christ all his life, rarely if ever missing a Sunday morning service. (In his 33 years with the Corps, he missed work just once, for an ear-ache, and retired with over two years of accrued sick leave.) He read a lot, both fiction and nonfiction. He liked fast cars, owning a Triumph TR4 followed by two Camaros. He enjoyed watching Formula 1 and Indy racing as well as Reds baseball and college football. Late in life, he took up vegetable gardening, which he pursued with scientific diligence, keeping detailed notes of conditions and results until he fell sick with cancer in the spring of 1989.

Genealogy was his last new hobby. He worked on it for just four years, making his last notes just after the birth of his namesake, John Tillman Mitchell IV, who would not have been so named had my father not succeeded in his search for his own first namesake, Jack Mitchell. He died at home the following year. May his memory be eternal!

Bibliography

Chalkley, Lyman, *Chronicles of the Scotch-Irish Settlement in Virginia: Extracted from the Original Court Records of Augusta County 1745–1800*, Vol. 1–3 (Mary S. Lockwood, 1912), https://archive.org/details/chroniclesscotc00lockgoog/page/n6/mode/2up.

Davis, William Watts Hart, *The History of Bucks County, Pennsylvania: From the Discovery of the Delaware to the Present Time* (Doylestown, Pa.: Democrat Book and Job Office, 1876).

Elliott, Katherine B., *Early Settlers of Mecklenburg County, Virginia* (Southern Historical Press, 2017).

Fischer, David Hackett, *Albion's Seed: Four British Folkways in America* (Oxford: Oxford University Press, 1989).

History of Cheatham County (Chicago and Nashville: The Goodspeed Publishing Co., 1887).

Leyburn, James G., *The Scotch-Irish: A Social History* (Chapel Hill, N.C.: The University of North Carolina Press, 1962).

Morton, Oren F., *A History of Rockbridge County, Virginia* (Staunton, Va., 1920; reprinted by Clearfield, 1994).

Rayback, Robert J., *Millard Fillmore: Biography of a President* (Newtown, Conn.: American Political Biography Press, 2009).

Reaney, P.H., *A Dictionary of English Surnames* (Oxford: Oxford University Press, Third Edition, 1997).

Rolleston, Mort, IV, "The Known Paternal Genealogy of My Georgia and Ballinamallard Rollestons," unpublished paper dated October 24, 2021.

Scarry, Robert J., *Millard Fillmore* (Jefferson, N.C.: McFarland, 2001).

Waddell, Jos. A., *Annals of Augusta County, Virginia, from 1729 to 1871*, (Staunton, Va.: C. Russell Caldwell, 1902).

About the Author

BRIAN PATRICK MITCHELL was born in Nashville, Tennessee, as were all his siblings. His father was also born in Nashville; his mother was born in Dickson. His grandparents were from Dickson, Cheatham, and Montgomery Counties. Brian earned his PhD in theology and an MTh in Orthodox studies from the University of Winchester and a BA in English literature from the University of Cincinnati. He is a proto-deacon of the Russian Orthodox Church, a former soldier and cabinet-level speechwriter, a former Washington bureau chief of *Investor's Business Daily*, and the author of several books and many articles on politics and religion, including an epic historical romance entitled *A Crown of Life* and an innovative work of political of theory entitled *Eight Ways to Run the Country*, which has been used to teach politics at Yale and elsewhere. His most recent book is *Origen's Revenge: The Greek and Hebrew Roots of Christian Thinking on Male and Female*, published in 2021 by Pickwick Publications, an imprint of Wipf and Stock. He blogs occasionally at brianpatrickmitchell.com.

www.ingramcontent.com/pod-product-compliance
Lightning Source LLC
Chambersburg PA
CBHW032356280326
41935CB00008B/598